Loui Schade

A Book for the Impending Crises!

Loui Schade

A Book for the Impending Crises!

ISBN/EAN: 9783337309787

Printed in Europe, USA, Canada, Australia, Japan

Cover: Foto ©Lupo / pixelio.de

More available books at **www.hansebooks.com**

A BOOK FOR THE "IMPENDING CRISIS!"

APPEAL

TO THE

COMMON SENSE AND PATRIOTISM

OF THE

PEOPLE OF THE UNITED STATES.

"HELPERISM" ANNIHILATED!

THE "IRREPRESSIBLE CONFLICT" AND ITS CONSEQUENCES!

BY LOUIS SCHADE, OF IOWA.

WASHINGTON, D C.
PUBLISHED BY LITTLE, MORRIS, & CO.,
AT THE OFFICE OF THE "NATIONAL DEMOCRATIC QUARTERLY REVIEW,"
NORTHWEST CORNER PENN. AV. AND SEVENTEENTH ST.
1860.

CONTENTS.

COMMON SENSE APPEAL

PEOPLE OF THE UNITED STATES.

INTRODUCTION.

Recent events—the treasonable and blood-shedding foray of John Brown into Virginia; the dissemination of incendiary volumes; the assertions of a leading politician and candidate for the Presidency in 1860, that the conflict between slavery and freedom is "irrepressible;" and the constant agitation of the slavery question by a party whose very existence depends upon a continued anti-slavery excitement, upon hatred and discord of one section of the country against the other—have brought the Union to the verge of dissolution, and are likely, if not checked in time, to destroy the grandest confederation that ever yet existed. The prosperity which we have enjoyed, the glory which the nation has achieved, the peace, security, and happiness, which hitherto have been our lot, are all imperilled by the divisions and dissensions, the animosities and heart-burnings, which already exist, and are daily engendered amongst us. The minds of the community have become hopelessly embittered and exasperated by long-continued irritation, so that the slightest occurrence will bring on the catastrophe. The war of words, of the press, of the State Legislatures, and, more than all, of the pulpit, has been pushed to a point of exasperation which, on the slightest untoward accident, may rush to the bloody arbitrament of the sword.

There are a great many and really humane men in the world who become agents of crime and disaster through ignorance of the consequences which must follow the initiatory steps of an acrimonious agitation; and of this class there are very many to be found in the

Northern and Eastern States, who would shrink with horror from any participation in the realities of a general uprising of one race against another, yet who would foster such undertakings as that of Brown, through ignorance what a negro insurrection really is. Brown's foray was nothing more and nothing less than an attempt to do on a vast scale what was done in St. Domingo in 1791, where the colored population was about equal to that of Virginia. For the information of this class of men, and all others who are uninformed as to the character of the African race when aroused, exasperated, and armed, the writer has taken pains to give, in the following pages, an accurate and true historical sketch of the negro revolution of St. Domingo. They will learn from the sober pages of history to what results their mistaken philanthropy will lead. They will find the ferocious and savage attributes of the negro character fearfully demonstrated. Let them, without prejudice, read the following pages. *Historia docet*, "history teaches," is an old Latin proverb, which never will lose its value and significance. The only wish of the writer is to do some good; to allay, if possible, the existing excitement on the slavery question, and bring back the former quietude and happiness, but especially a renewed love for the preservation of the Union, a strict obedience to the dictates of the Constitution, and an amicable state of feeling between the North and South. Although this work is more or less a reply to the Helper book, yet the writer has not the remotest idea to assume, in his arguments, sectional grounds. He is neither North nor South; he knows only one common country; and all his efforts are directed to procure happiness and content for the whole United States.

ST. DOMINGO.

The island of St. Domingo, or Hayti, extends about one hundred and forty miles in the broadest part from north to south, and three hundred and ninety from east to west. In a country of such magnitude, diversified with plains of vast extent, and mountains of prodigious height, is probably to be found every species of soil which nature has assigned to all the tropical parts of the earth. In general, it is fertile in the highest degree; everywhere well watered, and producing almost every variety of vegetable nature, for use and beauty, for food and luxury, which the lavish hand of a bountiful Providence has bestowed upon the richest portion of the globe. For beautiful scenery, richness of the soil, salubrity and variety of climate, it might justly be deemed the *Paradise of the New World*.

But here is no room for tracing the beauties of unsullied nature. The picture which I shall exhibit has nothing in it to delight the fancy or to gladden the heart. The prospects before us are all dark and dismal. Those groves of perennial verdure, those magnificent and romantic landscapes, which, in tropical regions, everywhere invite the eye, and oftentimes detain it, until wonder is exalted to devotion, must now give place to the miseries of war and the horrors of pestilence; to scenes of anarchy, desolation, and carnage. We have to contemplate the human mind in its utmost deformity; to behold savage man, let loose from restraint, exercising cruelties of which the bare recital makes the heart recoil, and committing crimes which are hitherto unheard of in history; teeming,

> ———" all monstrous, all prodigious things,
> Abominable, unutterable, and worse
> Than fables yet have feigned, or fear conceived !"—*Milton.*

Therefore, all that I can hope and expect is, that the following pages, if they cannot delight, may at least *instruct*. On the sober and considerate, on those who are open to conviction—in short, on all the honest, sincere masses of the Republican party, who still love the happiness and greatness of this country, abhor scenes of bloodshed and rapine, and desire to see the Union of these States exist for centuries to come—they cannot fail to leave a deep impression. The lamentable ignorance of some, and the monstrous wickedness of others, among the pseudo-philanthropists of the present day, will be exposed. It will be incontrovertibly proved that the rebellion of the negroes in St. Domingo, and the insurrection of the mulattoes, were caused by the very same means and agencies which are now employed by our Northern fanatics, and the Republican party in general, against the Southern States.

Causes which led to the Negro Rebellion at St. Domingo.

It has generally been conceded by all historians that the enslaved negroes in the French part of St. Domingo on the whole were treated with great leniency and indulgence. It has never been denied that the conduct of the whites towards them was in general similar to that of the masters towards their slaves in the United States. It was not the strong and irresistible impulse of human nature, groaning under oppression, that excited the negroes of Hayti to plunge their daggers into the bosoms of unoffending women and helpless infants. They were driven into those excesses—reluctantly driven—by the vile machinations of men calling themselves philosophers, whose pretences to philanthropy were a gross mockery of human reason, as their conduct was an outrage on all the feelings of our nature, and the ties which hold society together. Like those at Harper's Ferry, the slaves refused to join in the rebellion against their masters, until their African savage feelings, their cruel propensities, were aroused by the free mulattoes.

"There prevailed," says Mr. Edwards,[*] "at the commencement
' of the French Revolution, throughout the cities of France, a very
' strong and marked prejudice against the inhabitants of the sugar
' islands, on account of the slavery of their negroes. It was not
' indeed supposed, nor even pretended, that the condition of this
' people was worse at this juncture than in any former period; the
' contrary was known to be the truth. But declamations in sup-
' port of personal freedom, and invectives against despotism of all
' kinds, had been the favorite topics of many eminent French writers
' for a series of years; and the public indignation was now artfully
' raised against the planters of the West Indies. This spirit of
' hostility against the inhabitants of the French colonies was indus-
' triously fomented and aggravated by two associations, namely, the
' British Association for the Abolition of the Slave Trade, which
' held its meetings in the Old Jewry in London; and the society
' called *Les Amis des Noirs*, (Friends of the Blacks,) in Paris. A
' short review of the conduct of these societies will serve not only
' to lessen the surprise at the revolt of the negroes of St. Domingo,
' but also raise a considerable degree of astonishment that the
' enslaved negroes in the British islands had not given them the
' example."

"I have observed, that the society in London *professed* to have
' nothing more in view than to obtain an act of the Legislature for
' prohibiting the further introduction of African slaves into the Brit-
' ish Colonies. I have said that '*they disclaimed all intention of
' interfering with the government, and condition of the negroes
' already in the plantations; publicly declaring their opinion to*

_____

[*] Bryant Edwards, three volumes, published in 1801, an eye-witness of the Revolution of St. Domingo.

' be, that a general emancipation of those people, in their present
' state of ignorance and barbarity, instead of a blessing, would
' prove to them the source of misfortune and misery.' But although
' such were their ostensible declarations as a public body, the leading
' members of the society, in the same moment, held a very different
' language; and even the society itself (acting as such) pursued a line
' of conduct directly and immediately repugnant to their own profes-
' sions. Besides using every possible endeavor to inflame the public
' of Great Britain against the planters, they distributed, at a pro-
' digious expense, throughout the colonies, tracts and pamphlets with-
' out number, the direct tendency of which was to render the white
' inhabitants odious and contemptible in the eyes of their own slaves,
' and excite in the latter such ideas of their natural rights and equality
' of condition, as should lead them to a general struggle for freedom
' through rebellion and bloodshed. In many of those writings argu-
' ments are expressly adduced, in language which cannot be misunder-
' stood, to urge the negroes to rise up and murder their masters without
' mercy. ' Resistance,' say they, ' is always justifiable where force
' is the substitute of right; *nor is the commission of a civil crime*
' *possible in a state of slavery.*' (!!) These sentiments are repeated
' in a thousand different forms, and in order that they might not lose
' their effect by abstract reasoning, a reverend divine of the Church
' of England, in a pamphlet addressed to the chairman of the society,
' pours forth the most earnest prayers, in the most undisguised ex-
' pressions, that the negro would destroy all the white people, men,
' women, and children, in the West Indies. ' Should we not,' he
' exclaims, ' approve their conduct in their violence? Should we
' not crown it with eulogium, if they exterminate their tyrants with
' fire and sword. *Should they even deliberately inflict the most*
' *exquisite tortures on those tyrants, would they not be excusable*
' in the moral judgment of those who properly value those inesti-
' mable blessings, rational and religious liberty?' "*

We perceive that the Beechers, Cheevers, Wendell Phillipses,
were not wanting at that time! How similar are their expressions
against slavery! How anxious and eager are they—those pious
ministers of the Gospel—to incite, in spite of these dismal historical
facts, a rebellion of our negroes! One might think that their
"philanthropical" sentiments and feelings could not be satisfied
and quieted, until, like their worthy predecessors, they have heard
the wailing cry of the butchered infant, or seen the white mother,
after the most demoniacal tortures, breathe her last in the arms of
savage Africans! But let Mr. Edwards continue:

"Besides distributing pamphlets of this complexion *gratis* at the

* This is a fair extract from a letter addressed to Granville Sharp, Esq., chairman of the society in the Old Jewry, by the Rev. Percival Hockdale, A. M. Of
such writers, the planters may well exclaim, " *Forgive them; they know not what*
they do."

' doors of all the churches and places of worship in the Kingdom,
' (England,) and throughout the colonies, the society, or persons in
' their name, caused a medal to be struck, containing the figure of
' a naked negro, loaded with chains, and in the attitude of imploring
' mercy; thousands of which also were dispersed among the negroes
' in each of the sugar islands, for the instruction, I presume, of such
' of them as could not read.   But this instance of provident caution
' was hardly requisite; for so many negro domestics return annually
' from Europe to the West Indies, as constantly furnish a sufficient
' number of living instructors; and certain it is (I pronounce it from
' my own knowledge respecting Jamaica) that the labors of the soci-
' ety on their behalf, as *well as many of the most violent speeches*
' *in the British Parliament*, WHEREIN THE WHOLE BODY OF PLANT-
' ERS WERE PAINTED AS A HERD OF BLOOD-THIRSTY AND REMORSE-
' LESS TYRANTS, were explained to the negro slaves in terms well
' adapted to their capacities, and suited, as might have been sup-
' posed, to their feelings.   It will be difficult to say what other
' measures the Old Jewry associates could have taken to excite a
' rebellion, except that of furnishing the objects of their solicitude
' with firearms and ammunition.

  " Hitherto, this society had served as a model and exemplar to
' that of Paris; but a disposition to stop at half measures consti-
' tutes no part of the French character; and the society of *Amis*
' *des Noirs* resorted, without scruple, to those measures which their
' fellow laborers in London still hesitated to adopt.   Besides, having
' secretly in view to subvert the ancient despotism of the French
' Government, they loudly clamored for a general and immediate
' abolition, not only of the slave trade, but also of the slavery which
' it supported.   Proceeding on abstract reasoning, rather than on
' the actual condition of human nature, they distinguished not be-
' tween civilized and uncivilized life, and considered that it ill be-
' came them to claim freedom for themselves, and withhold it at
' the same time from the negroes.   It is to be lamented that a prin-
' ciple so plausible in appearance, should, in its application to this
' case, be visionary and impracticable.   They began with the class
' of free mulattoes, because they found many of them in France,
' who became the willing instruments of their purposes, and who
' undertook to interpret to the negroes in the French colonies the
' wishes and good intentions towards them of their friends in the
' mother country.   Hitherto, between the free mulattoes and the
' negro slaves, a bitter hatred and envy had existed.   It was the
' mulattoes themselves who were the hard-hearted task-masters to
' the negroes, a great many of them being in possession of fine planta-
' tions, and owning slaves themselves.   Thus an opening was made
' towards conciliation and union between the two classes.   The
' negroes, believing that it was only through the agency of the
' mulattoes, and the connections of those people in France, they

' could obtain a regular supply of arms and ammunition, forgot or
' suspended their ancient animosities; and the men of color, sensi-
' ble that nothing but the co-operation of the enslaved negroes
' (docile as they supposed them to be, from their ignorance, and
' irresistible from their numbers) could give success to their cause,
' courted them with such an assiduity as gained over at least nine-
' tenths of all the slaves in the northern province of St. Domingo.''

For general information, it may be well to state here, that at that
time the total number of whites amounted to about 80,000 ; that
of the free colored people, or mulattoes, to 24,000 ; and that of the
negro slaves to 480,000—about sixteen colored persons against one
white man.

" As already mentioned, a considerable body of the mulattoes
' from St. Domingo and the other French islands were resident, at
' this juncture, in the French capital. Some of these were young
' people, sent thither for education; others were men of considerable
' property. With these people, the Society of *Amis des Noirs*
' formed an intimate connection, pointed out to them the wretched-
' ness of their condition, filled the nation with remonstrances and
' appeals on their behalf, and poured out such invectives against the
' white planters, as bore away reason and moderation in the torrent.
' The personal appearance of the mulattoes excited pity, and, co-
' operating with the temper of the times and credulity of the French
' nation, raised such an indignant spirit in all ranks of people against
' the white colonists, as threatened their total annihilation and ruin.

" In this disposition of the people of France towards the inhab-
' itants of their colonies in the West Indies, the National Assem-
' bly voted the celebrated *declaration of rights*. Happy had it
' been for the general interests of the human race, if, when the
' French had gone thus far, they had proceeded no farther ! Happy
' for themselves, if they had then known—what painful experience
' has since taught them—that the worst of all Governments is pref-
' able to the miseries of anarchy ! To promulgate such lessons and
' doctrines in the colonies, as the declared sense of the Supreme
' Government, was to subvert the whole system of their establish-
' ments. Accordingly, a general ferment prevailed among the
' French inhabitants of St. Domingo, from one end of the colony to
' the other. All that had passed in the mother country concerning
' the colonists—the prejudices of the metropolis towards them, the
' efforts of the society of *Amis des Noirs* to emancipate the ne-
' groes, and the conduct of the mulattoes—had been represented to
' them through the medium of party, and perhaps with a thousand
' circumstances of exaggeration and insult, long before the declara-
' tion of rights was received in the colony ; and this measure crowned
' the whole. They maintained that it was calculated to convert their
' *peaceful and contented negroes into implacable enemies*, and ren-
' der the whole country a theatre of commotion and bloodshed.''

In the mean, while, the French Government, apprehensive that disorders of a very alarming nature might arise in the colonies from the proceedings in France, had issued orders to the Governor General of St. Domingo to convoke the inhabitants for the purpose of forming a legislative assembly for interior regulation. These orders, however, being unaccountably delayed, the people had anticipated the measure. The inhabitants of the northe district had already constituted a Provincial Assembly, which met a Cape François, and their example was followed in November in the western and southern provinces. All assemblies agreed that there should be a full and speedy colonial representation, and if within three months they should not have received instructions from the King for calling such an assembly, the colony should take on itself to adopt and enforce the measure; their immediate safety and preservation being, they said, an obligation paramount to all others.

" During this period of anxiety and alarm, the mulattoes (free
' colored people) were not inactive. Instructed by their brethren in
' the metropolis in the nature and extent of their rights, and ap-
' prised of the favorable disposition of the French nation towards
' them, they became, throughout the colony, actuated by a spirit of
' turbulence and sedition, and, disregarding all considerations of
' prudence with regard to time and seasons, determined to claim,
' without delay, the full benefit of all the privileges enjoyed by the
' whites. Accordingly, large bodies of them appeared in arms, in
' different parts of the country; but, acting without sufficient concert
' or due preparation, they were easily overpowered. It is said that
' the temper of the Provincial Assemblies at this juncture, how much
' soever inflamed against the instigators and abettors of these people
' in the mother country, was *not* averse to moderation and conces-
' sion towards the mulattoes themselves! Thus, when the party
' which had taken arms at Jacmel was defeated, and their chiefs
' imprisoned, the Assembly of the West (Port-au-Prince) interposed
' with effect in favor of the whole number; and at Artibonite, where
' the revolt was much more extensive and alarming, a free and un-
' conditional pardon was also cheerfully granted, on the submission
' of the insurgents ! "

This will clearly prove that it was not cruelty on the part of the whites that induced the free mulattoes to revolt !

" Against such of the whites, however, as had taken any part in
' these disturbances in favor of the people of color, the rage of the
' populace knew no limits. Mons. Dubois, deputy *procureur gen-
' er al*, had not only declared himself an advocate for the mulattoes,
' but, with a degree of imprudence which indicated insanity, sought
' occasions to declaim publicly against the slavery of the negroes. The
' Northern Assembly arrested his person, and very probably intend-
' ed to proceed to greater extremities; but the Governor interposed
' in his behalf, obtained his release, and sent him from the country.

" Mons. Ferrand de Beaudierre, who had formerly been a magis-
' trate at Petit Goave, was not so fortunate. This gentleman was
' unhappily onamored of a woman of color, to whom, as she possessed
' a valuable plantation, he had offered marriage; and being a man
' of warm imagination, with little judgment, he undertook to combat
' the prejudices of the whites against the whole class. He drew
' up, in the name and behalf of the mulatto people, a memorial to the
' parochial committee, wherein, among other things, they were made
' to claim, in express words, the full benefit of the national Decla-
' ration of Rights. Nothing could be more ill-timed or injudicious
' than this proceeding; it was evident that such a claim led to con-
' sequences of which the mulattoes themselves (who certainly at
' this juncture had no wish to enfranchise the slaves) were not ap-
' prised. This memorial therefore was considered as a summons to
' the negroes for a general revolt. The parochial (county) commit-
' tee seized the author, and committed him to prison; but the popu-
' lace took him from thence by force, and in spite of the magistrates
' and municipality, who exerted themselves to stop their fury, put
' him to death."

The King's order for convoking a General Colonial Assembly
was received in St. Domingo early in the month of January, 1790.
It appointed the town of Leogane for the place of meeting; and instructions accompanied the order, concerning the mode of electing
the members. These instructions, however, being considered by the
provincial assemblies as inapplicable to the circumstances of the
colony, were disapproved; and another plan, better suited to the
wealth, territory, and number of the inhabitants, was adopted.

" In the mean while, intelligence was received in France of the
' temper of St. Domingo towards the mother country. The inhab-
' itants were very generally represented as manifesting a disposition
' either to renounce their dependency, or to throw themselves under
' the protection of a foreign Power; and the planters of Martinique
' were said to be equally discontented and disaffected. The trading
' and manufacturing towns took the alarm; and petitions and re-
' monstrances were presented from various quarters, (Union meet-
' ings?) imploring the National Assembly to adopt measures for
' composing the minds of the colonists, and preserving to France its
' most valuable dependencies.

" On the 8th of March, 1790, the French National Assembly en-
' tered, indeed, into the consideration of the subject, with a serious-
' ness and solemnity suited to its importance; and, after full discus-
' sion, a very large majority voted ' that it never was the intention
' of the Assembly to comprehend the interior government of the
' colonies in the Constitution which they had framed for the mother
' country, or to subject them to laws which were incompatible with
' their local establishments; they therefore authorize the inhabit-
' ants of each colony to signify to the National Assembly their sen-

' timents and wishes concerning that plan of interior legislation and
' commercial arrangement, which would be most conducive to their
' prosperity.' It was required, however, that the plan to be offered
' should be conformable to the principles which had connected the
' colonies with the metropolis, and be calculated for the preser-
' vation of their reciprocal interests. To this decree was annexed
' a declaration, ' That the National Assembly would not cause any
' innovation to be made, directly or indirectly, in any system of com-
' merce in which the colonies were already concerned.'

  " Nothing could equal the clamor which this decree occasioned
' among the people of color resident in France, and the philanthropic
' society of *Amis des Noirs*, (Friends of the Blacks.) The decla-
' ration concerning commerce was interpreted into a tacit sanction
' for the continuance of the slave trade. It was even said that the
' colonists were no longer subject to the French empire, but mem-
' bers of an independent State. Nevertheless, if the circumstances
' of the times and the disposition of the French colonists at this
' juncture be taken into the account, candor must acknowledge that
' it was a decree not only justifiable on the motives of prudence and
' policy, but was founded also on the strong basis of moral neces-
' sity. The arguments that were urged against it seem to imply
' that the benefits of the French Revolution were intended only for
' the people residing in the realm, in exclusion of their fellow-sub-
' jects in the plantations. After that great event, to suppose that
' the inhabitants of those colonies (with the successful example, too,
' of the English-Americans recent in their memories) would have
' submitted to be governed and directed in their local concerns by a
' legislature at the distance of 8,000 miles from them, is to mani-
' fest a very slender acquaintance with human nature."

  The General Assembly of St. Domingo met on the 16th of April,
1790. One of their first measures was to relieve the people of color
from the hardships to which they were subject under the military
jurisdiction. It was decreed that in future no greater duty should
be required of them in the militia than from the whites; and the
harsh authority, in particular, which the King's lieutenants, majors,
and other officers commanding in the towns, exercised over those
people, (free colored,) was declared oppressive and illegal. The Assembly, however, having expressed too much spirit of independence,
as far as the authority of the mother country was concerned, Governor Peynier, who was merely waiting for an opportunity to return
to the ancient *regimé*, being a royalist at heart, issued a proclamation to dissolve the same. He charged the members with entertain-
ing projects of independency, and pronounced them, and all their
adherents, traitors to their country, and enemies to the nation and
the King. Several skirmishes ensued. A large force was collected
by the Governor in the western province, under the command of
Col. *Mauduit*, commandant of the Port-au-Prince regiment. A

stop, however, was put to the immediate shedding of blood, by the sudden and unexpected determination of the General Assembly to undertake a voyage to France, and justify their conduct to the King and the National Assembly in person. Accordingly, eighty-five of the members (of whom sixty-four were fathers of families) actually embarked on board the Leopard, and, on the 8th of August, took their departure for Europe—a proceeding which created as much surprise in the Governor and his party, as admiration and applause among the people at large. Persons of all ranks accompanied the members to the place of embarkation, pouring forth prayers for their success, and shedding tears of sensibility and affection for a conduct which was generally considered as noble a proof of self-denial, and as signal an instance of heroic virtue and Christian forbearance, as any age has exhibited. A momentary calm followed this event; the parties in arms appeared mutually disposed to submit their differences to the King and the French Assembly. Such was the issue of the first attempt to establish a free Constitution in the French part of St. Domingo, on the system of a limited monarchy.

Rebellion of James Ogé, (John Brown.)

From the first meeting of the General Assembly of St. Domingo, to its dissolution and dispersion, the colored people (meaning always the free colored) remained, on the whole, more peaceable and orderly than might have been expected. The temperate and lenient disposition manifested by the Assembly towards them produced a beneficial and decisive effect in the western and southern provinces; and, although three hundred of them from these provinces had been persuaded by Col. Mauduit to join the forces under his command, they very soon became sensible of their error, and, instead of marching towards St. Marc, as Mauduit proposed, they demanded and obtained their dismission, and returned quietly to their respective habitations. (The reader will bear in mind that the 480,000 negro slaves at this time never stirred; the 24,000 free colored people alone composed the unruly part.)

Such of the mulatto people, however, as resided at that juncture in France, continued in a far more hostile disposition. They were encouraged in their animosity towards the white colonists by parties of very different descriptions. The colonial decree of the 28th of May, 1790, (which prescribes that the inhabitants of the colony shall have the exclusive right to make all laws concerning their own domestic affairs, including slavery,) was no sooner made known in France, than it excited universal clamor. Many persons, who agreed in nothing else, united their voices in reprobating the conduct of the inhabitants of St. Domingo. The adherents of the ancient regime were joined on this occasion by the partisans of democracy and republicanism. These two factions hoped to obtain very different ends by the same means. And there was another party who exerted themselves with equal assiduity in promoting public confusion. These were the discordant class of speculative reformers, every one of them having probably formed a favorite system of freedom which he was eager to recommend to others. The philanthropic society called *Amis des Noirs*, strengthened by such auxiliaries, was more powerful than ever; and it is not surprising that the efforts of this society should have operated strongly on the minds of those mulattoes who were taught to consider their personal wrongs as the cause of the nation, and have driven some of them into the wildest excesses of fanaticism and fury.

" Among such of these unfortunate people resident in France as
' were thus inflamed into madness, was a young man, under thirty
' years of age, named James Ogé. He was born in St. Domingo, of a
' mulatto woman who still possessed a coffee plantation. He had
' been introduced to the meetings of the *Amis des Noirs*, under the
' patronage of Gregoire, Brissot, and Robespierre, the leading mem-
' bers of that society, and was by them initiated into the popular
' doctrine of *equality* and the *rights of man*. These persons, how-
' ever, had other objects in view. Their aim was, not to reform,
' but to destroy—to excite convulsions in every part of the French
' empire; and the ill-fated Ogé became the tool, and was afterwards
' the victim, of their guilty ambition.

" He had been led to believe," [like Brown,] " that the whole
' body of colored people in the French islands were prepared to rise
' up as one man against their masters; that nothing but a discreet
' leader was wanting to set them into action; and, fondly conceiv-
' ing that he possessed in his own person all the qualities of an able
' general, he determined to proceed to St. Domingo by the first op-
' portunity. To cherish the conceit of his own importance, and
' animate his exertions, the society procured him the rank of lieu-
' tenant colonel in the army of one of the German electors.

" As it was found difficult to export a sufficient quantity of arms
' and ammunition from France without attracting the notice of the
' Government, and awakening suspicion among the planters resident
' in the mother country, the society resolved to procure those arti-
' cles in the United States, and it was recommended to Ogé to make
' a circuitous voyage for that purpose. Accordingly, being furnished
' with money and letters of credit, he embarked for New England
' (!) in the month of July, 1790.

" But, notwithstanding the caution that was observed in this in-
' stance, the whole project was publicly known at Paris previous to
' Ogé's embarkation, and notice of the scheme, and even a portrait
' of Ogé himself, was transmitted to St. Domingo long before his
' arrival in that island. He secretly landed there, from an Amer-
' ican sloop, on the 12th October, 1790, and found means to convey
' undiscovered the arms and ammunition which he had purchased in

' tho United States to tho place which his brother had prepared for
' their reception.

" The first notice which the white inhabitants received of Ogé's
' arrival, was from himself. He dispatched a letter to the Governor,
' (Peynier,) wherein, after reproaching the Governor and his prede-
' cessors with the non-execution of the *code noir*, he demanded, in
' very imperious terms, that the provisions of that celebrated statute
' should be enforced throughout the colony. He required, also, that
' the privileges enjoyed by one class of inhabitants (the whites)
' should be extended to all persons, without distinction, (not inclu-
' ding herein, however, the four hundred and eighty thousand negro
' slaves, but the free mulattoes, of whom many were slaveholders
' themselves,) declaring himself the protector of the mulattoes, and
' announcing his intention of taking up arms in their behalf, unless
' their wrongs should be redressed.

" About six weeks had intervened between the landing of Ogé
' and the publication of this mandate, in all which time he and his
' two brothers had exerted themselves to the utmost in spreading dis-
' affection and exciting revolt among the mulattoes. Assurances
' were held forth, that all the inhabitants of the mother country
' were disposed to assist them in the recovery of their rights, and
' it was added, that the King himself was favorably inclined to their
' cause. Promises were distributed to some, and money to others.
' But, notwithstanding all these efforts, and that the temper of the
' times was favorable to his views, Ogé was not able to allure to his
' standard above two hundred followers; and of these, the major
' part were raw and ignorant youths, unused to discipline, and averse
' to all manner of subordination and order.

" He established his camp at a place called Grande Riviere,
' about fifteen miles from Cape François, and appointed his two
' brothers, together with one Mark Chavane, his lieutenants. Cha-
' vane was fierce, intrepid, active, and enterprising, prone to mis-
' chief, and thirsty for vengeance. Ogé himself, with all his enthu-
' siasm, was naturally mild and humane. He cautioned his followers
' against the shedding innocent blood, but little regard was paid
' to his wishes in this respect. The first white man that fell in their
' way they murdered on the spot; a second, of the name of Sicard,
' met the same fate; and it is related that their cruelty towards such
' persons of their own complexion as refused to join in the revolt
' was extreme. A mulatto man of some property, being urged to
' follow them, pointed to his wife and six children, assigning the
' largeness of his family as a motive for wishing to remain quiet.
' This conduct was considered contumacious, and it is asserted that
' not only the man himself, but the whole of his family, were mas-
' sacred without mercy.

" Intelligence was no sooner received at the town of Cape Fran-
' çois of these enormities, than the inhabitants proceeded with the

2

' utmost vigor and unanimity, to adopt measures for suppressing the
' revolt.   A body of regular troops, and the Cape regiment of mili-
' tia, were forthwith dispatched for that purpose.   They soon in-
' vested the camp of revolters, who made less resistance than might
' have been expected from men in their desperate circumstances.
' The rout became general; many of them were killed, and about
' sixty made prisoners; the rest dispersed themselves in the moun-
' tains.   Ogé himself, one of his brothers, and Chavane, his asso-
' ciate, took refuge in the Spanish territories.   Of Ogé's other
' brother, no intelligence was ever afterwards obtained.

   " After this unsuccessful attempt of Ogé, and his escape from
' justice, the disposition of the white inhabitants in general towards
' the mulattoes was sharpened into great animosity.   The lower
' classes, in particular, (those whom the colored people call *les petits*
' *blancs*,) breathed nothing but vengeance against them, and very
' serious apprehensions were entertained, in all parts of the colony,
' of a proscription and massacre of the whole body.

   " Alarmed by reports of this kind, and the appearances which
' threatened them from all quarters, the mulattoes flew to arms in
' many places.   They formed camps at different places, but the
' largest and most formidable body assembled near the little town,
' Verette.   The white inhabitants collected themselves in consider-
' able force in the neighborhood, and Colonel Mauduit, (the French
' commanding officer,) with a corps of two hundred men from the
' regiment of Port-au-Prince, hastened to their assistance, but
' neither party proceeded to actual hostility.   Mons. Mauduit even
' left his detachment at the port of St. Marc, thirty-five miles from
' Verette, and proceeding singly and unattended to the camp of the
' mulattoes, had a conference with the leaders.   What passed on
' that occasion was never publicly divulged.   It is certain that the
' mulattoes retired to their habitations in consequence of it; but the
' silence and secrecy of Mons. Mauduit, and his influence over them,
' gave occasion to very unfavorable suspicions, by no means tending
' to conciliate the different classes of the inhabitants to each other.
' He was charged with having traitorously persuaded them not to
' desist from their purpose, but only to postpone their vengeance to
' a more favorable opportunity; assuring them, with the utmost
' solemnity and apparent sincerity, that the King himself, and
' all the friends of the ancient Government, were secretly attached
' to their cause, and would avow and support it whenever they could
' do it with advantage, and that the time was not far distant, etc.
' He is said to have pursued the same line of conduct at Jeremie,
' Les Cayes, and all the places he visited.   Everywhere, he held
' secret consultations with the chiefs of the mulattoes, and those
' people everywhere immediately dispersed.   At Les Cayes, a
' skirmish had happened before his arrival there, in which about
' fifty persons on both sides lost their lives, and preparations were

' making to renew hostilities. The persuasions of Mons. Mauduit
' effected a truce; but Rigaud, the leader of the mulattoes in that
' quarter, openly declared that it was a transient and deceitful calm,
' and that no peace would be permanent until one class of people
' had exterminated the other.

"In November, 1790, Mons. Peynier resigned the Government, and
' embarked for Europe. The first measure of Mons. Blanchelande,
' the new commander-in-chief, was to make a peremptory demand
' of Ogé and his associates from the Spaniards; and the manner in
' which it was enforced induced an immediate compliance therewith.
' The wretched Ogé, and his companions in misery, were delivered
' over, the latter end of December, to a detachment of French
' troops, and safely lodged in the jail of Cape François, with the
' prisoners previously taken, and a commission was afterwards issued
' to bring them to trial. Twenty of Ogé's deluded followers, among
' them his own brother, were condemned to be hanged. To Ogé
' himself, and his lieutenant, Chavane, a more terrible punishment
' was allotted; they were adjudged to be broken alive, and left to
' perish in that dreadful situation on the wheel. The bold and
' hardened Chavane met his fate with unusual firmness, and suffered
' not a groan to escape him during the extremity of his tortures;
' but the fortitude of Ogé deserted him altogether. When sentence
' was pronounced, he implored mercy with many tears and an
' abject spirit. He promised to make great discoveries if his life
' was spared, declaring that he had an important secret to commu-
' nicate. A respite of twenty-four hours was accordingly granted;
' but it was not made known to the public, at that time, that he
' divulged anything of importance. It was discovered, however,
' about nine months afterwards, that this unfortunate young man
' had not only made a full confession of the facts already related,
' but also disclosed the dreadful plot in agitation. His last solemn
' declarations and dying confession, sworn to and signed by himself
' the day before his execution, were actually produced, wherein he
' details at large the measures which the colored people had fallen
' upon to *excite the negro slaves to rise into rebellion!* He points
' out the chiefs by name, and relates that, notwithstanding his own
' defeat, a general revolt would actually have taken place in the
' month of February preceding, if an extraordinary flood of rain,
' and consequent inundation from the rivers, had not prevented it.
' He declares that the ringleaders still maintained the same atro-
' cious project, and held their meeting in certain subterranean pas-
' sages, or caves, in the parish of La Grande Riviere, to which he
' offers, if his life might be spared, to conduct a body of troops, so
' that the conspirators might be secured."

The commissioners before whom this confession was made, being
devoted adherents to the Bourbons, suppressed or disregarded Ogé's
narrative, and hurried him to immediate execution, seemingly to

prevent the further communication and full disclosure of so weighty a secret.

Thus ended, the most important outbreak of the rebellion at St. Domingo. Till now, the 480,000 negro slaves had taken no active part. They had remained quiet and undisturbed by what was going on around them. The free colored people, impelled by the French societies, and aiming at equal political rights with the whites, had alone constituted the revolutionary element. And even they would have kept quiet, if outside influences, especially those philanthropical societies, would have permitted them. Besides these, strong efforts were made by the royalists in the colony as well as by the republican party at Paris to incite bloodshed and strife for their particular purposes.

Decree of the National Assembly (at Paris) of the 15th May, 1791.

The eighty-five members of the General Assembly of St. Domingo arrived at Brest (France) on the 13th September, 1790. They were received on landing by all ranks of people with congratulations and shouts of applause. The same honors were shown to them as would have been paid to the National Assembly. Their expenses were defrayed, and sums of money raised for their future occasions, by a voluntary and very general subscription. But these testimonies of respect and kindness served only to increase the disappointment which they soon afterwards experienced in the capital, where a very different reception awaited them. Agents of Peynier and Mauduit, also of the Provincial Assembly of the north, were already arrived, and had so effectually prevailed with Mons. Barnave, the President of the Committee for the Colonies, that they found their cause prejudged, and their conduct condemned without a hearing. On the 21st of September, the National Assembly issued a peremptory order, directing them to attend at Paris, and wait their further directions. Their prompt obedience to this order procured them no favor. They were allowed a single audience only, and then indignantly dismissed from the bar. They solicited a second, and an opportunity of being confronted with their adversaries. The National Assembly refused their request, and directed the Colonial Committee to hasten its report concerning their conduct. On the 11th of October, this report was presented by M. Barnave. It comprehended a detail of all the proceedings of the Colonial Assembly, and censured their general conduct in terms of great asperity, representing it as flowing from motives of disaffection towards the mother country. The report concluded by recommending "that ' all the pretended decrees and acts of the said Colonial-Assembly ' should be reversed, and pronounced utterly null and of no effect; ' that the said Assembly should be declared dissolved, and its mem- ' bers rendered ineligible and incapable of being delegated in future ' to the Colonial Assembly of St. Domingo; that the King should

' be requested to give orders for the forming of a new Colonial
' Assembly, on the principles of the national decree of the 8th of
' March, 1790, and instructions of the 28th of the same month;
' finally, that the *ci-devant* members, then in France, should con-
' tinue in a state of arrest until the National Assembly might find
' time to signify its further pleasure concerning them." A decree
to this effect was accordingly voted on the 12th of October, by a
very large majority, and the King was requested at the same time
to send out an augmentation of force; both naval and military, for
the better supporting the regal authority in St. Domingo.

None can describe the surprise and indignation which the news of
this decree excited in St. Domingo, except among the partisans of
the monarchical Government. By them it was regarded as the first
step towards the revival of the ancient system. By most other persons it was considered as a dereliction, by the National Assembly,
of all principles; and the orders for electing a new Colonial Assembly were so little regarded, that many of the parishes positively
refused to choose other deputies until the fate of their former members—at that time in France—should be decided; declaring that
they still considered those persons as the legal representatives of
the colony. One immediate and apparent effect of this decree was
to heighten and inflame the popular sentiment against Mauduit and
his regiment, who had been the instruments in preparing this unhappy state of affairs. Even two new French regiments, which
arrived in March, 1791, from France, perceiving that hostile disposition towards Mauduit's regiment by the National Guards, and the
people in general, refused all manner of communication and intercourse with the soldiers of the same, and even declined to enter into
any of their places of amusement. This conduct in the new comers
towards the ill-fated regiment soon made a wonderful impression on
the minds both of officers and privates of the regiment itself. Mauduit, soon perceiving the full extent of his dangers from his own
grenadiers, told them that he was willing, for the sake of peace, to
restore to the National Guards the colors which he formerly (when
dissolving the General Assembly) had taken from them, and even
to carry them, with his own hands, at the head of his regiment,
and deposit them in the church in which they had been usually
lodged. The next day the ceremony took place, and Mauduit restored the colors, before a vast crowd of spectators. At that moment,
one of his own soldiers cried aloud, *that he must ask pardon of
the national troops on his knees,* and the whole regiment applauded
the proposal. Mauduit started back with indignation, and offered
his bosom to their swords; it was pierced with a hundred wounds,
all of them inflicted by his own men, while not a single hand was
lifted up in his defence.

While these shameful enormities were passing in St. Domingo,
the society of *Amis des Noirs* in the mother country were but too

successfully employed in devising projects which gave birth to deeds of still greater horror, and produced scenes that transformed the most beautiful colony in the world into a field of desolation and carnage.

Although it must have occurred to every unprejudiced mind, from the circumstances that have been related concerning the behaviour of the mulattoes residing in the colony, that the general body of those people were by no means averse to conciliation with the whites, yet it was found impossible to persuade their pretended friends in Europe to leave the affairs of St. Domingo to their natural course. Barnave alone (hitherto the most formidable opponent of the colonists) avowed his conviction that any further interference of the mother country in the question between the whites and the colored people would be productive of fatal consequences. Such an opinion was entitled to greater respect, as coming from a man who, as President of the Colonial Committee, must be supposed to have acquired an intimate knowledge of the subject; but he was heard without conviction. There are enthusiasts in politics as well as in religion, and it commonly happens, with fanatics in each, that the recantation of a few of their number serves only to strengthen the errors and animate the purposes of the rest. It was now resolved, by Gregoire, Brissot, and some others, to call in the supreme legislative authority of the French Government.

The decree of the 8th of March, 1790, which gave to the colonists the right to legislate in their internal affairs, was accompanied by a code of instructions for the Governor, for its due and punctual observance and execution. The code contained, among other things, a direction "that every person of the age of twenty-five and upwards, ‘ possessing property, or having resided two years in the colony, and ‘ paid taxes, should be permitted to vote in the formation of the ‘ Colonial Assembly."

Every one of the friends of the colonists in the Assembly had not the least doubt that only white persons were meant by the phrase " every person." The framers and supporters of the measure pretended that it went only to the modification of the privilege of voting in the parochial meetings, which, it was well known, under the old Government, had been constituted of white persons only. The colored people had in no instance attended those meetings, nor set up a claim, or even expressed a desire, to take any part in the business transacted thereat. But these instructions were no sooner adopted by the National Assembly, and converted into a decree, than its framers and supporters threw off the mask, and the mulattoes resident in France, as well as the society of *Amis des Noirs*, failed not to apprise their friends and agents in St. Domingo, that the people of color, not being excepted, were virtually comprised in it. These, however, not thinking themselves sufficiently powerful to enforce the claim, or perhaps doubting the real meaning of the decree, sent deputies to France to demand an explanation of it from the National Assembly.

In the beginning of May, 1791, the consideration of this subject was brought forward by Abbé Gregoire, and the claim of the free mulattoes to the full benefit of the instructions of the 28th of March, 1790, and to all the rights and privileges enjoyed by the white inhabitants, was supported with all that warmth and eloquence for which he was distinguished. Unfortunately, at this juncture, the news of the miserable death of Ogé arrived at Paris, and raised a storm of indignation in the minds of all ranks of people, which the planters resident in France were unable to resist. Nothing was heard in all companies but declamations against their oppression and cruelty. To support and animate the popular outcry against them, a tragedy or pantomime, formed on the story of Ogé, was represented in the public theatres. By these and other means, the planters became so generally odious, that for a time they dared not to appear in the streets of Paris. These were the arts by which Gregoire, Condorcet, Brissot, and Robespierre, disposed the public mind to clamor for a new and explanatory decree, in which the rights of the free colored people should be placed beyond all future doubts and dispute. The friends and advocates of the planters were overpowered and confounded. In vain did they predict the utter destruction of the colonies, if such a proposal should pass into a law. "Perish the colonies," said Robespierre, "rather than sacrifice one iota of our principles." The majority reiterated the sentiment, and the famous decree of the 15th of May, 1791, was pronounced amidst the acclamation and applause of the multitude.

By this decree it was declared and enacted, "That the people ' of color residing in the French colonies, born of free parents, ' were entitled to, as of right, and should be allowed the enjoyment ' of, all the privileges of French citizens, and, among others, to ' those of having votes in the choice of representatives, and of *being* ' *eligible to seats both in the Parochial and Colonial Assemblies.*" Thus did the National Assembly sweep away in a moment all the laws, usages, prejudices, and opinions, concerning these people, which had existed in the French colonies from their earliest settlement, and tear up by the roots the first principle of a free Constitution—*the sole and exclusive right of a people of passing laws for their local and interior regulation and government.* The Colonial Committee, of which Mons. Barnave was chairman, failed not to apprise the National Assembly of the fatal consequences of this measure, and immediately suspended the exercise of its functions. At the same time, the deputies from the colonies signified their purpose to decline any further attendance.

Consequences in St. Domingo of the Decree of the 15*th of May. First Rebellion of the Negro Slaves. The " Irrepressible Conflict" Doctrine carried out.*

I am now to enter on the retrospect of scenes, the horrors of which imagination cannot adequately conceive, nor pen describe. The disputes and contests between different classes of French citizens, and the violences of malignant factions, claim no longer attention. Such a picture of human misery, such a scene of woe, presents itself, as no other country, no former age, has exhibited. Upwards of one hundred thousand savage people, habituated to the barbarities of Africa, avail themselves of the silence and obscurity of the night, and fall on the peaceful and unsuspicious planters, like so many famished tigers, thirsting for human blood. Revolt, conflagration, and massacre, everywhere mark their progress; and death, in all its horrors, or cruelties and outrages, compared to which immediate death is mercy, await alike the old and the young, the matron, the virgin, and the helpless infant. No condition, age, or sex, is spared. All the shocking and shameful enormities with which the fierce and unbridled passions of man have ever conducted a war, prevail uncontrolled. The rage of fire consumes what the sword is unable to destroy, and in a few dismal hours the most fertile and beautiful plains in the world are converted into one vast field, of carnage—a wilderness of desolation!

The decree of the 15th of May was the brand by which the flames were lighted, and the combustibles that were prepared set into action. Intelligence having been received of it at Cape François on the 30th of June, no words can describe the rage and indignation which immediately spread throughout the colony. The inhabitants now unanimously determined to reject the civic oath, although great preparations had been made for a general federation on the 14th of July. The news of this decree seemed to unite the most discordant elements. The national cockade was everywhere trodden under foot, and the Governor General, who continued a sorrowful and silent spectator of these excesses, found his authority annihilated in a moment. In a memorial, which he afterwards published, concerning his administration, he says: " Acquainted with the genius and tem-
' per of the white colonists, by a residence of seven years in the
' Windward Islands, and well informed of the grounds and motives
' of their prejudices and opinions concerning the people of color, I
' immediately foresaw the disturbances and dangers which the news
' of this ill-advised measure would inevitably produce; and not
' having it in my power to suppress the communication of it, I lost
' no time in apprising the King's Ministers of the general discon-
' tent and violent fermentation which it excited in the colonies.
' To my own observations, I added those of many respectable, sober,
' and dispassionate men, whom I thought it my duty to consult in

' so critical a conjuncture; and I concluded my letter by expressing
' my fears that this decree would prove the death-warrant of many
' thousands of the inhabitants. The event has mournfully verified
' my predictions ! ''

In the mean while, so great was the agitation of the public mind,
that Mons. Blanchelande, the Governor, found it necessary not only
to transmit to the Provincial Assembly of the North a copy of the
letter which he had written to the King's Ministers, but also to accompany it with the solemn assurance *to suspend the execution of
the obnoxious decree, whenever it should come out to him properly
authenticated ;* a measure which too plainly demonstrated that his
authority in the colony was at an end.

" Justly alarmed at all these proceedings, so hostile towards their
' pretended rights, and probably apprehensive of a general proscrip-
' tion, the mulattoes throughout the colony began to collect in dif-
' ferent places in armed bodies; and the whites, by a mournful fatal-
' ity, suffered them to assemble without molestation. In truth,
' every man's thoughts were directed towards the meeting of the
' new Colonial Assembly, from whose deliberations and proceedings
' the extinction of party, and the full and immediate redress of all
' existing grievances, were confidently expected. Besides, the decree
' furnished the mulattoes with a plausible cause for resorting to
' arms. The strong tide of popular prejudice which prevailed in
' the mother country against the planters, and the great majority
' which voted for the fatal decree in the National Assembly, com-
' bined with constant exhortations of the philanthropical societies
' both in England and France, were circumstances that inspired
' them with so dangerous a confidence in their own resources, as
' overpowered all considerations of prudence and humanity. It is
' natural that the enslaved negroes could not possibly be unob-
' servant of these combined and concurred circumstances. They
' beheld the colored people in open hostility against the whites.
' They were assured that the former had the fullest support and
' encouragement from the supreme legislature of the mother coun-
' try. They were taught to believe that they also had become ob-
' jects of the paternal solicitude of the King and the National As-
' sembly, who wished to rescue them from the dominion of their
' masters, and invest them with their estates. It appeared, from
' indisputable evidence, that assurances of this nature were held out
' to the enslaved negroes. Whoever shall calmly deliberate on these
' and the other facts that have been stated, will find no difficulty in
' accounting for the dreadful extent of this insurrection, or in as-
' signing to its proper cause, and tracing to the fountain-head, those
' rivers of blood which have been flowing in that unfortunate and
' devoted colony.''

It was on the morning of the 23d of August, 1791, just before
day, that a general alarm and consternation spread throughout the

town of the Cape. The inhabitants were called from their beds by persons who reported that all the negro slaves in the several neighboring parishes had revolted, and were at that moment carrying death and desolation over the adjoining large and beautiful plain to the northeast. The Governor and most of the military officers on duty assembled together, but the reports were so confused and contradictory as to gain but little credit. As daylight began to break, the sudden and successive arrival, with ghastly countenances, of persons who had with difficulty escaped the massacre, and flown to the town for protection, brought a dreadful confirmation of the fatal tidings.

" The rebellion first broke out on a plantation called *Noé*, in the ' parish of Acul, nine miles only from the city. Twelve or fourteen ' of the ringleaders, about the middle of the night, proceeded to the ' refinery, or sugar-house, and seized on a young man, the refiner's ' apprentice, dragged him to the front of the dwelling-house, and ' there hewed him into pieces with their cutlasses; his screams ' brought out the overseer, whom they instantly shot. The rebels ' now found their way to the apartment of the refiner, and massacred ' him in his bed. A young man lying sick in a neighboring cham-' ber was left apparently dead of the wounds inflicted by their ' cutlasses. He had strength enough, however, to crawl to the next ' plantation, and relate the horrors he had witnessed. He reported ' that all the whites of the estate which he had left were murdered, ' except only the surgeon, whom the rebels had compelled to accom-' pany them, on the idea that they might stand in need of his pro-' fessional assistance. Alarmed by this intelligence, the persons to ' whom it was communicated immediately sought their safety in ' flight.

" The revolters (consisting now of all the slaves belonging to that ' plantation) proceeded to the house of a Mr. Clement, by whose ' negroes also they were immediately joined, and both he and his ' refiner were massacred. The murderer of Mr. Clement was his ' own postillion, (coachman,) a man to whom he had always shown ' great kindness. The other white people on this estate contrived ' to make their escape.

" At this juncture, the negroes on the plantation of M. Faville, ' a few miles distant, likewise rose and murdered five white persons, ' one of whom (the attorney for the estate) had a wife and three ' daughters. Three unfortunate women, while imploring for mercy ' of the savages on their knees, beheld their husband and father ' murdered before their faces. For themselves, they were devoted ' to a more horrid fate, and were carried away captives by the as-' sassins.

" The approach of daylight served only to discover sights of hor-' ror. It was now apparent that the negroes on all the estates in ' the plain acted in concert, and a general massacre of the whites ' took place in every quarter. On some few estates, indeed, the

' lives of the women were spared, but they were reserved only to
' gratify the brutal appetites of the ruffians ; and it is shocking to
' relate, *that many of them suffered violation on the dead bodies of*
' *their husbands and fathers !*

 " In the town itself, the general belief for some time was, that
' the revolt was by no means an extensive, but a sudden and partial
' insurrection only. The largest sugar plantation on the plains was
' that of Mons. Gallifet, situated about eight miles from the town,
' the negroes belonging to which had always been treated with such
' kindness and liberality, and possessed so many advantages, that it
' became a proverbial expression among the lower white people, in
' speaking of any man's good fortune, to say, *il est heureux comme*
' *un negre de Gallifet,* (he is as happy as one of Gallifet's negroes.)*
' Mons. Odeluc, the attorney or agent for this plantation, was a mem-
' ber of the General Assembly, and, being fully persuaded that the
' negroes belonging to it would remain firm in their obedience, de-
' termined to repair thither to encourage them in opposing the in-
' surgents, to which end he desired the assistance of a few soldiers
' from the town guard, which was granted him. He proceeded· ac-
' cordingly, but, on approaching the estate, to his surprise and grief,
' he found all the negroes in arms on the side of the rebels, and
' (horrid to tell !) THEIR STANDARD WAS THE BODY OF A WHITE
' INFANT, WHICH THEY HAD RECENTLY IMPALED ON A STAKE !
' Mons. Odeluc had advanced too far to retreat undiscovered, and
' both he and a friend that accompanied him, with most of the
' soldiers, were killed without mercy. Two or three of the patrol
' escaped by flight, and conveyed the dreadful tidings to the inhab-
' itants of the town."

 By this time, all or most of the white persons that had been
found on the several plantations, being massacred or forced to seek
their safety in flight, the ruffians exchanged the sword for the torch.
The buildings and cane-fields were everywhere set on fire, and the
conflagrations, which were visible from the town in a thousand different quarters, furnished a prospect more shocking and reflections
more dismal than fancy can paint or the powers of man describe.

 "Consternation and terror now took possession of every mind,
' and the screams of the women and children, running from door to
' door, heightened the horrors of the scene. All the citizens took up
' arms, and the General Assembly vested the Governor with the
' command of the National Guards, requesting him to give such
' orders as the urgency of the case seemed to demand. One of the

---

*The Hon. Mr. Everett stated the same fact in his great speech at the Boston
Union meeting. The Abolitionists have since tried to pervert the meaning of those
words, by insinuating that Gallifet treated his negroes so badly that the above
expressions are used ironically. My authority, however, is older than that of the
Abolitionists ; I quote literally from a book published in 1801, by a gentleman
who visited Hayti at the beginning of the rebellion.

' first measures was to send the white women and children on board
' the ships in the harbor; very serious apprehensions being enter-
' tained concerning the domestic negroes within the town, a great
' proportion of the ablest men among them were likewise sent on
' shipboard and closely guarded.

"There still remained in the city a considerable body of free
' mulattoes who had not taken, or affected not to take, any part in
' the disputes between their brethren of color and the white inhabit-
' ants.   Their situation was extremely critical; for the lower class
' of whites, considering the mulattoes as the immediate authors of
' the rebellion, marked them for destruction; and the whole number
' in the town would undoubtedly have been murdered without scru-
' ple, had not the Governor and the Colonial Assembly vigorously
' interposed, and taken them under their immediate protection.
' Grateful for this interposition in their favor, (perhaps not thinking
' their lives otherwise secure,) all the able men among them offered
' to march immediately against the rebels, and to leave their wives
' and children as hostages for their fidelity.   Their offer was accept-
' ed, and they were enrolled in different companies of the militia."

The Assembly continued their deliberations throughout the night,
amidst the glare of surrounding conflagrations.   The inhabitants,
being strengthened by a number of seamen from the ships, and
brought into some degree of order and military subordination, were
now desirous that a detachment should be sent out to attack the
strongest body of the revolters.   Orders were given accordingly,
and Mons. de Touzard, an officer who had distinguished himself in
the United States service, took the command of a party of militia
and troops of the line.   With these he marched to the plantation
of Mons. Latour, and attacked a body of about four thousand of the
rebel negroes.   Many were destroyed, but to little purpose; for
Touzard, finding the number of revolters to increase to more than
a centuple proportion of their losses, was at length obliged to retreat.
The Governor, by the advice of the Assembly, now determined to
act for some time solely on the defensive; and, as it was every
moment to be apprehended that the revolters would pour down upon
the town, all the roads and passes leading into it were fortified.
At the same time, an embargo was laid on all the shipping in the
harbor—a measure of indispensable necessity, calculated as well to
obtain the assistance of the seamen as to secure a retreat for the
inhabitants in the last extremity.

To such of the distant parishes as were open to communication,
either by land or by sea, notice of the revolt had been transmitted
within a few hours after advice of it was received at the Cape, and
the white inhabitants of many of those parishes had therefore found
time to establish camps, and form a chain of posts, which for a short
time seemed to prevent the rebellion spreading beyond the northern

province.* Two of these camps, however, were attacked by the
negroes, (who were here openly joined by the mulattoes,) and forced
with great slaughter. At Dondon the whites maintained the contest for seven hours, but were overpowered by the infinite disparity
of numbers, and compelled to give way, with the loss of upwards of
one hundred of their body. The survivors took refuge in the Spanish territory.

These two districts, therefore—the whole of the rich and extensive plain of the Cape—together with the contiguous mountains,
were now wholly abandoned to the ravages of the enemy, and the
cruelties which they exercised on such of the miserable whites as
fell into their hands cannot be remembered without horror, nor
reported in terms strong enough to convey a proper idea of their
atrocity.

" They seized Mr. Blen, an officer of the police, and having NAIL-
' ED HIM ALIVE to one of the gates of his plantation, chopped off his
' limbs one by one with an axe.

"A poor man named Robert, a carpenter by trade, endeavoring
' to conceal himself from the notice of the rebels, was discovered in
' his hiding-place. The savages declared *that he should die in the
' way of his occupation.* Accordingly they bound him between two
' boards, and deliberately *sawed him asunder.*

" Mons. Cardineau, a planter of Grande-Riviere, had two natural
' sons by a black woman. He had manumitted them in their in-
' fancy, and bred them up with great tenderness. They both joined
' in the revolt, and when their father endeavored to divert them
' from their purpose by soothing language and pecuniary offers, they
' took his money, and then stabbed him to the heart.

" All the white and even the mulatto children, whose fathers had
' not joined in the revolt, were murdered without exception, *fre-
' quently before the eyes or clinging to the bosoms of their mothers.*
' Young women of all ranks were first violated by a whole troop of
' barbarians, and then generally put to death. Some of them were
' indeed reserved for the further gratification of the lust of the sav-
' ages, and others had their eyes scooped out with a knife.

" In the parish of Limbé, at a place called the Great Ravine, a
' venerable planter, the father of two beautiful young ladies, was
' tied down by a savage ringleader of a band, who ravished the eld-
' est daughter *in his presence,* and delivered over the youngest to
' one of his followers. Their passion being satisfied, they slaughter-
' ed both the father and the daughters."

In the frequent skirmishes between the foraging parties sent out
by the negroes (who, after having burnt down everything, were in

---

* It is believed that a general insurrection was to have taken place throughout
the whole colony on the 25th day of August, but the impatience and impetuosity
of some negroes on the plain induced them to commence their operations two days
before that time.

scarcity of provisions) and the whites, the rebels seldom stood their ground longer than to receive and return one single volley, but they appeared again the next day; and though they were at length driven out of their entrenchments with infinite slaughter, yet their numbers seemed not to diminish. As soon as one body was cut off, another appeared, and thus they succeeded in the object of harassing and destroying the whites by perpetual fatigue, and reducing the country to a desert.

To detail the various conflicts, skirmishes, massacres, and scenes of slaughter, which this exterminating war produced, were to offer a disgusting and frightful picture—a combination of horrors, wherein we should behold cruelties unexampled in the annals of mankind; human blood poured forth in torrents; the earth blackened with ashes, and the air tainted with pestilence. It was computed that, *within two months after the revolt first began, upwards of two thousand white persons, of all conditions and ages, had been massacred; that one hundred and eighty sugar plantations, and about nine hundred coffee, cotton, and indigo settlements, had been destroyed, (the buildings thereon being consumed by fire,) and one thousand two hundred Christian families reduced from opulence to such a state of misery as to depend altogether for their clothing and sustenance on public and private charity! Of the insurgents, it was reckoned that upwards of ten thousand had perished by the sword or by famine, and some hundreds by the hands of the executioner!!*

Are the people of the United States prepared for such horrid scenes of devastation, atrocities, and bloodshed, in their midst? Will they profit from these unhappy experiences, or is the "irrepressible-conflict" doctrine to be carried out in this country in a similar manner? Will they follow the teachings of those philanthropical fools, some of them perhaps under pay from England, who talk without thinking, and promulgate abstract ideas of liberty and equality, without calculating their necessary consequences and results if carried out? Let all true patriots and friends of humanity ponder on these trist facts!

The flames of rebellion soon began to break forth also in the western division. Here, however, the insurgents were chiefly men of color, of whom upwards of two thousand appeared in arms in the parish of Mirabalais. Being joined by about six hundred of the negro slaves, they began their operations by burning the coffee plantations in the mountains. Some detachments of the military, which were sent against them from Port-au-Prince, were repulsed, and the insurgents continued to ravage and burn the country through an extent of thirty miles, practicing the same excesses and ferocious barbarities towards such of the whites as fell into their hands, as were displayed by the rebels in the north. They had the audacity at length to approach Port-au-Prince, with intention of setting it on fire. So defenceless was the state of that devoted town, that its destruction seemed inevitable. Many of the mulatto chiefs, however, finding that their attempts *to gain over the negro slaves on the sugar plantations* in this part of the country were not attended with that success which they expected, expressed an unwillingness to proceed to this extremity, declaring that they took up arms, not to desolate the colony, but merely to support the national decree of the 15th of May, and that they were not averse to a reconciliation. These sentiments coming to the knowledge of Mons. de Jumecourt, a planter of eminence, he undertook the office of mediator; and through his influence a truce called the *concordat* was agreed upon the 11th of September, between the free people of color and the white inhabitants of Port-au-Prince, of which the chief provisions were, an oblivion of the past, and an engagement, on the part of the whites, to admit in full force the national decree of the 15th of May, certainly the ostensible, though perhaps not the sole and original, cause of rebellion. Thus peace was once more restored. All would have been well, if only outside influences would have ceased to be used to stir up commotion and strife in the unfortunate country.

But let us return to France, where we left Gregoire, Robespierre, and the rest of the society of *Amis des Noirs*, exulting in the triumph they had obtained on the 15th of May, and perhaps waiting that their obnoxious decree would produce those very evils which actually resulted from it. It was not until the beginning of September that information arrived at Paris concerning the reception which the account of this decree had met with in St. Domingo. The tumults, disorders, and confusions, that it produced there, were now represented in the strongest coloring, and the loss of the colony to France was universally apprehended. At this time, however, no suspicion was entertained concerning the enslaved negroes; but a civil war between the whites and mulattoes was believed to be inevitable. The commercial and manufacturing towns, predicting the ruin of their trade and shipping, and the loss of their capital from existing dangers, presented remonstrances and petitions to the National Assembly, urging the necessity of an immediate repeal of all the decrees by which the rights of the planters were invaded—that of the 15th of May especially. The constituent National Assembly was now on the point of dissolution, and perhaps wished to leave everything in peace. At the same time, the tide of popular prejudice, which had hitherto ran with such violence against the colonists, was beginning to turn. Most of those members whose opinions in colonial concerns a few months before had guided the deliberations of the National Assembly, were now either silently disregarded, or treated with contempt. At length, a motion was made to annul the obnoxious decree, and (strange to tell!) *on the 24th of September its repeal was actually voted by a large majority !*—thirteen days after the *concordat* or truce between the white inhabitants of Port-au-Prince and the mulattoes had been established, and peace restored! It will be remembered that the *concordat* recognised all the rights and privileges conferred by the decree of the 15th of May upon the free colored people.

To such repugnancy and absurdity must every Government be driven, that attempts to regulate and direct the local concerns of a country three thousand miles distant. It is difficult to say which of the two measures produced the greatest calamity—the decree of the 15th of May in the first instance, or its unexpected repeal at the time and in the manner mentioned! Doubts had already arisen in the minds of the mulattoes concerning the sincerity and good faith of the white people with respect to the *concordat*. Their suspicions and apprehensions had indeed grown to such a height as to induce them to insist on a renewal and confirmation of its provisions, which were accordingly granted to them by a new instrument, or treaty, of the 11th of October. But no sooner was authentic information of the repeal of the decree received from France, than all trust and confidence, and every hope of reconciliation and amity between the two classes, vanished forever. It was impossible to persuade the mulattoes that the planters in the colony were innocent and ignorant of the transaction. They accused the whites of the most horrid duplicity, faithlessness, and treachery, and publicly declared that one party or the other, themselves or the whites, must be utterly destroyed and exterminated. *There was no longer*, they said, *an alternative*. The "irrepressible-conflict" doctrine was once more brought into operation!

Open war, and war in all its horrors, was now renewed. All the soft workings of humanity, all the compunctious visitings of nature, were now absorbed in the raging and insatiable thirst of revenge, which inflamed each class alike. It was no longer a contest for mere victory, but a diabolical emulation which party could inflict the most abominable cruelties on the other. The enslaved negroes in the district Cul-de-sac joined the mulattoes—a bloody engagement took place, in which the negroes (the slaves) being ranged in front, and acting without any kind of discipline, left two thousand of their number dead on the field. Of the mulattoes, about fifty were killed and several taken prisoners. The whites claimed the victory, but for want of cavalry were unable to improve it by a pursuit, and contented themselves with satiating their revenge on their captives. But, in order to prevent misunderstandings, it will be here proper to state that the whites comprised in their ranks not only the "slaveholders," but French soldiers and the non-slaveholding white population. The whole white race was in arms.

" The mulattoes scorned to be outdone in deeds of vengeance and ' atrocities shameful to humanity. In the neighborhood of *Jeremie*, ' a body of them attacked the house of Mons. Léjourné, and secured ' the persons both of him and his wife. This unfortunate woman—

‘ my hand trembles while I write—was far advanced in her preg-
‘ nancy. The monsters, whose prisoner she was, having first mur-
‘ dered her husband in her presence, *ripped her up alive, and threw*
‘ *the infant to the hogs. They then (how shall I relate it?) sewed*
‘ *up the head of the murdered husband in* —————*!!!* Such are thy
‘ triumphs, philanthropy! And such an act was committed by
‘ mulattoes, some of whom had received an education in France!
‘ What may have been the deeds of the untaught negro slaves ! ’’

With justice may we exclaim, of our Abolition and Republican
leaders, who are now busily engaged in preparing the advent of such
horrid scenes—the impending crisis, as they style it—in our own
midst, "*Forgive them; they know not what they do!*"—or if they
do, they are the greatest —————; but everybody can answer that for
himself.

With these enormities terminated the disastrous year 1791. Just
before Christmas, the three civil commissioners nominated by the
National Assembly for St. Domingo, arrived at Cape François.
Much was expected from their appointment by the friends of peace
and good order, but the sequel will show that they effected very
little towards restoring the peace of the country.

The commissioners of the National Assembly arrived in September from France. They proclaimed a general amnesty and pardon
to all who should desist from acts of insubordination, and who would
subscribe to the new Constitution. This proposition was disapproved by the Colonial Assembly, and by all parties. The commissioners then left the Island, in which they found themselves
powerless and disrespected. By the white inhabitants, a general
amnesty to the men of color and revolted slaves was considered as a
justification of the most horrible atrocities, and as holding out a
dangerous example to such of the negroes as preserved their fidelity.
The mulattoes received the decree of the commissioners with contempt and indignity, as it annulled their favorite decree of the 15th
of May. At *Petit Goave*, the free colored persons were masters,
and held in close confinement thirty-four white persons, whom they
reserved for vengeance. On the publication of this amnesty, they
led them to execution; but, instead of putting them to immediate
death, they caused each of them to be broken alive, and, in the
midst of their tortures, read to them, in a strain of diabolical mockery, the proclamation, affecting to consider it as a pardon for the
cruelties they had just committed.

The Society of *Amis des Noirs* had soon attained considerable
influence in the National Assembly. On the 29th of February,
1792, Garan de Coulon, after a long and inflammatory harangue
against the planters in general, proposed a decree for abrogating
that of the 24th of September, declaring a general amnesty throughout all the French colonies, and granting to all free colored persons
the right of suffrage, and of being eligible to the Legislature and

places of trust; enacting that new Colonial Assemblies should be formed, which should transmit their sentiments, not only on the subject of the internal government of the colonies, but also *on the best method of effecting the abolition of negro slavery in toto.* Frantic as the new Legislature had shown itself on many occasions since its first meetings, a majority could not at this time be found to vote for so senseless and extravagant a proposition. But a short time afterwards, this Assembly passed the famous decree of the 4th April, 1792.

The carrying of this decree into effect was intrusted to three commissioners—Santhonax, Polverel, and Ailhaud—who, with a force of 8,000 men, arrived at St. Domingo on the 13th of September following. They immediately dissolved the Colonial Assembly, and sent the Governor (Blanchelande) to France, where he was tried and guillotined. Mons. Desparbes, his successor, having disagreed with the commissioners, was suspended and sent to France, where he was, it is said, also guillotined.

It was asserted by the whole inhabitants that the commissioners of the National Assembly, while professing to the white inhabitants their earnest solicitude for the preservation of the peace and the prosperity of the colony, were secretly intriguing with the mulattoes; and they, in the end, openly declared that the latter, with the free negroes, should enjoy their civil privileges, and the protection of the 8,000 National Guards which had arrived from France. The commissioners held secret communications with the chiefs of the mulattoes, in all parts of the colony. Besides, they sent a great number of whites in a state of arrest to Europe, to answer before the National Assembly to the accusations which they pretended to transmit against them. Among the persons thus imprisoned and transported to France, were comprehended the colonel, lieutenant colonel, and many other officers of the Cape regiment.

A new Governor, Mons. Galbaud, arrived in May, 1793, to take the command, and to place the Island in a state of defence, in case the British might invade it, war having been declared between the two Powers. The National Assembly of France soon after sent out commissioners with fresh instructions, and suspended the new Governor. They decreed that any person holding property in the colonies should be ineligible to fill any office of trust in the colony in which his estate was situated.

Galbaud, aided by his brother, armed a force, composed of militia, seamen from the ships in the harbor of Cape Haytien, (François,) and a great number of volunteers, and marched without delay against the commissioners, who were with the regular troops. A bloody conflict ensued, and the battle was continued with obstinate bravery, until the sailors, who composed the greatest strength of Galbaud's force, became disorderly. He was consequently obliged to retreat. Various skirmishes followed. Galbaud's brother fell into the hands of the commissioners, and the son of one of the commissioners was captured by Galbaud.

But a scene now opens, which, if it does not obliterate, exceeds at least all that has hitherto been related of factious anarchy and savage cruelty in this unfortunate colony. The commissioners, finding that their troops were rapidly deserting, and that Galbaud's forces were resolute, and fighting with unexampled bravery, called to their aid the revolted slaves, offering them their freedom, and promising them the pillage of the city of Cape Haytien, then called Cape François. Some of the rebel chiefs rejected this dishonorable proposition; but Macaya, a negro of brutal disposition, with an insatiable thirst for the blood of the whites, accepted the proposal of the commissioners, and with 3,000 or 4,000 of the negroes joined the commissioners. The city was attacked, and men, women, and children, were without distinction slaughtered. The white inhabitants fled from all sides to the seaside, in hopes of finding shelter with the Governor on board the ships in the harbor; but a body of mulattoes cut off their retreat, and a hurried butchery ensued, which continued with unremitting fury from the 21st of June to the evening of the 23d, when the savages, having murdered all the white inhabitants that fell in their way, set fire to the buildings. More than half the city was consumed by the flames. The mulattoes had now acquired the utmost power of gratifying their revenge; they even sacrificed their own white parents, and afterwards subjected their bodies to every species of insult and indignity. Every white person was bayoneted or cut down—*except the young females, who were in most cases spared for the gratification of the lust of those into whose hands they fell!* Some of the most delicate and beautiful of the female sex were brought forth to witness the butchery of their parents and relatives; and they were afterwards subjected to the vile embraces of the executioner. Even girls of twelve and fourteen years were made the victims of lust and revenge. Such massacre and rapine as those committed in the revolution of St. Domingo are almost unequalled in the annals of atrocity. So terrible were the excesses, that the commissioners themselves repaired to the ships, from which they were spectators of the effects of their own crimes, and beheld an opulent city consumed by the flames, and the inhabitants subjected to the most atrocious massacre. Such was the fate of the once flourishing and beautiful capital of St. Domingo!—a city which, for trade, opulence, and magnificence, was undoubtedly among the first in the West Indies.

After the destruction of the beautiful city of Cape François, and the massacre of most of the white inhabitants, emigrations commenced from the colony to the United States, to the neighboring islands, and of some of the opulent planters to England, under the impression that the British Government would be disposed to turn its attention to their cause. The war between France and England having commenced, the Government of England sent directions to the Governor of Jamaica to afford to those inhabitants of St. Domingo, who were desirous of placing themselves under British protection, every possible support, and to send without delay a competent force to take possession of such places as the people might be disposed to surrender to them.

The intentions of the British Government being known by means of secret agents, the commissioners of the National Assembly "proclaimed the abolition of every species of slavery, declaring that ' the negroes were thenceforth to be considered as free citizens." From this moment, the colony was lost to Europe and to civilization; the dominion of African barbarism was extended over the most beautiful country on the globe. For though but few of the negroes in proportion to the whole joined the commissioners—many thousands choosing to continue slaves as they were, and participate in the fortunes of their masters—yet vast numbers in all parts of the colony (apprehensive probably that this offer of liberty was too great a favor to be permanent) availed themselves of it to secure a retreat to the mountains, and possess themselves of the natural fastnesses within. They then sallied forth into the plains, and set fire to the cane-fields, demolishing every habitation within their range, and murdering the white inhabitants. In one part of Hayti, the insurgents amounted to nearly one hundred thousand, without any resolute leader.

The principal object of the writer—to prove by historical facts that it was not the enslaved negroes who commenced the rebellion in St. Domingo, but that all the unfortunate disturbances and frightful atrocities arose from the interference and agitation of outside influences, especially from the constant and untiring machinations of those so-called philanthropical societies in England and France—has been attained. It will not be necessary for his purpose to give a detailed sketch of the revulsions which followed the invasion of the English, and their disastrous expulsion; neither will I mention the various attempts of the French to subjugate the Island, and reduce it again to the dominion of France. But it may be, perhaps, not improper to make a few remarks on what the colony was before the revolution broke out.

Statistics of Hayti.

The French part of St. Domingo, comprising about one-third of the whole Island, was in the highest state of prosperity in 1790. The quantity of land in cultivation was 2,289,480 English acres, of which about two-thirds were situated in the mountains. There were 792 sugar, 2,860 coffee, 705 cotton, 3,097 indigo, 69 cocoa plantations, on which 480,000 negroes were employed. The white population amounted, in 1790, to 30,831 (exclusive of European troops and sea-faring people.) The number of mulattoes and other free colored people was estimated at 24,000.

The exterior appearance of the colony everywhere demonstrated great and increasing prosperity. Cultivation was making rapid advances over the country. The towns abounded in warehouses, which were filled with the richest commodities and productions of Europe, and the harbors were crowded with shipping. There were freighted in 1787, for Europe alone, 470 ships, containing 112,253 tons, and navigated by 11,220 seamen. The exportations to France from the 1st of January, 1791, to the 31st of December of the same year, were:

Products.		Quantities.	Value in livres.
Sugar, (white,) pounds	- - -	70,227,708	67,670,781
" (brown) "	- - -	93,177,512	49,041,567
Coffee, "	- - -	68,151,180	51,890,748
Cotton, "	- - -	6,286,126	17,572,252
Indigo, "	- - -	930,016	10,875,120
Cocoa, "	- - -	150,000	120,000
Syrup, jars	- - -	29,502	1,947,132
Tafia, kegs	- - -	803	21,816
Hides, (tanned,) sides	- - -	7,887	78,870
" (raw,) number	- - -	5,186	93,348
Tortoise-shell, pounds	- - -	5,000	50,000
Mahogany and Campeche, pounds	-	1,500,000	40,000

Value in colonial currency (livres)	- - -	199,401,634
Value in dollars	- - - - - -	$27,828,000

The total value of agricultural property, including negroes, stock, etc., in 1790, is stated at about $208,297,000.

The following table exhibits the general decline in the production of sugar, coffee, cotton, and indigo, between the years 1789 and 1826. In 1789, Hayti was a colonial possession of France; in 1801, it was under the government of Toussaint; in 1818 and 1819, it was under that of Christophe; and during the residue of the years designated in the statement, it was under that of President Boyer:

Exports from Hayti.

Years.	Sugar.		Coffee.	Cotton.	Indigo.
	White. Pounds.	Brown. Pounds.	Pounds.	Pounds.	Pounds.
1789 - -	47,516,531	93,573,300	76,835,219	7,004,274	758,628
1801 - -	16,540	18,518,572	43,420,270	2,480,340	804
1818 - -	198	5,443,567	26,065,200	474,118	—
1819 - -	157	3,790,143	29,240,919	216,103	—
1820 - -	2,787	2,514,502	35,137,759	346,839	—
1821 - -	—	600,934	29,925,951	820,563	—
1822 - -	—	200,454	24,235,372	592,368	—
1823 - -	—	14,920	33,802,837	332,256	—
1824 - -	—	5,106	44,269,084	1,028,045	1,240
1825 - -	—	2,020	36,034,300	815,697	—
1826 - -	—	32,864	32,189,784	620,972	—

The following statement exhibits the quantities of cotton, coffee, cocoa, logwood, and tobacco, exported from Hayti from 1835 to 1849:

Years.	Coffee Pounds.	Cotton. Pounds.	Cocoa. Pounds.	Logwood. Pounds.	Tobacco. Pounds.
1835	48,325,371	1,649,717	397,321	13,293,737	2,086,606
1840	46,126,272	922,575	442,365	39,283,205	1,725,389
1845	41,002,571	537,480	836,004	68,181,588	5,609
1846	33,508,179	570,061	630,102	59,933,868	576
1847	48,388,699	525,083	1,171,520	32,795,670	—
1848	37,630,435	411,463	905,895	36,340,072	—
1849	30,608,343	544,126	664,516	86,232,580	—

A glance at the statements will show that a great change took place in the character of the exportation from Hayti during the sixty years between 1789 and 1849. Sugar, indigo, and tobacco, which were staples of export in 1789, had entirely disappeared from the table in 1849. The exportation of coffee had been reduced to less than one-half; that of cotton had also greatly diminished.

In view of these statistics, it is evident that the movement of the country has been vastly retrograde since it was a possession of France. In 1789, it exported 150,000,000 pounds of sugar, and nearly 1,000,000 pounds of indigo; in 1849, it exported none. In the former years it exported 77,000,000 pounds of coffee, and more than 7,000,000 pounds of cotton. In 1849, the exportation of the former amounted to less than 31,000,000 pounds, and of the latter to little more than 500,000 pounds; while the total value of exportations from Hayti, which, in 1789, are given at 205,000,000 francs, were, forty years later, but 3,500,000 francs! A foreign resident at the capital of Hayti, in view of these facts, writes as follows, under recent date:

" This country has made, since its emancipation, no progress
' whatever. The population partially live upon the produce of the
' grown-wild coffee plantations, remnants of the French dominion.
' Properly speaking, plantations after the model of the English in
' Jamaica, or the Spanish in Cuba, do not exist here. Hayti is the
' most beautiful and the most fertile of the Antilles. It has more
' mountains than Cuba, and more space than Jamaica. Nowhere
' the coffee-tree could better thrive than here, as it especially likes
' a mountainous soil. But the indolence of the negroes has brought
' the once splendid plantations to decay. They now gather the
' coffee only from the grown-wild trees. The cultivation of the
' sugar-cane has entirely disappeared; and the island that once
' supplied one-half of Europe with sugar, now supplies its own
' wants from Jamaica and the United States."

Whatever our philanthropists will say to the contrary, the negro is incapable of self-government. He is incapable, by his own exertions, to advance in civilization. If left to himself, he always will fall back into his former state of African barbarism. Mazeres, in

speaking of them, says: "The negro is only a grown child, shal-
' low, light, fickle, thoughtless, neither keenly sensible of joy nor of
' sorrow, improvident, without resources in his spirits or his soul.
' Careless, like other sluggards ; rest, singing, his women, and his
' dress, form the contracted limits of his taste. I say nothing of
' his affections, for affections, properly so called, are too strong for
' a soul so soft, so inactive as his."

It is true, that under Toussaint, Dessalines, and Christophe, the
exportations of Hayti were still considerable. But were the negroes free? Was it by their free will that they went to work? By
no means! They were in a worse state of slavery than before,
under the French Government. Toussaint knew the character and
the disposition of his negro brethren too well ; he was aware that
only by force they would be induced to labor. The system adopted
by him was not dissimilar to that which prevails in Russia, where
the peasantry are "*adscripti glebæ.*" The planters were compelled to employ them as servants; and the negroes were ordered to
choose the employers under whom they were to work, and on no consideration were they allowed to leave the estates on which they agreed to
labor, unless their services were demanded in the army. He fixed
wages for the laborers, to be computed equal to one-third of the value
of the crops. Military guards were placed to superintend the laborers, and to seize those who endeavored to evade their duty. There
were no civil authorities by which the indolent or refractory cultiva-
tor was to be tried for his offences ; there was no distinction between
the vagrant who was detected in idleness and the soldier who fled
from his post ; they were both amenable to the military power, were
sentenced by a court martial, and awarded an equal punishment.

Dessalines followed in the footsteps of Toussaint. He knew that,
by making his negroes work, he could procure the necessary money.
In order to increase the male population, he wished to enter into a
treaty with the British agent from Jamaica, "*offering to open the
' ports of Hayti to the British slave ships, and to grant to the
' Jamaica importers the exclusive right of selling negroes in
' Hayti!*" He wanted them particularly for the cultivation of the
Government lands, which had fallen, from neglect, into a state of
unproductiveness. Christophe, like his predecessors, knew also
well that if he were to relax authority, and if the people were left
to their own free agency, from their innate love of indolence, nothing
could be obtained of them. They would wander about, quite un-
concerned for to-morrow, satisfied with that which the day produced.
He knew that the negro race were prone to idleness, and addicted
to lust and sensuality ; that they were ignorant of the duties of
civilized life, and of the ties which bound them together. With
these impressions, Christophe and his Council, and other advisers,
set about a work, which, however imperfect they may be considered
as legislators, exhibits no little share of judgment. His "*Code*

Henri" appeared in 1812. Some of its laws are new; those of agriculture and commerce are decidedly such as were in force in the time of Toussaint and Dessalines. In short, the negroes were nominally free, but actually as much slaves, and in some respects, perhaps, more so, than under the French dominion.

From the day on which Christophe expired, down to the present day, neither improvement, nor energetic administration, nor the extension of the education of the people, nor any progress in the march of civilization, appears in the agricultural, manufacturing, commercial, moral, social, or political condition of the Republic of Hayti. The climate, the soil, and the pastures, yield, almost without culture, sufficient merely to feed a people too indolent to work for comforts and luxuries. In short, Hayti, the paradise of the West Indies, the most fertile and beautiful country in this hemisphere, is at present the Africa of the New World. If in possession of white people, its great resources and agricultural riches would nourish and enrich millions of happy people; but now they hardly suffice to let the barbarian negro enjoy the pleasures, vices, and indolence, of his savage ancestors. The rebellion of 1791, instead of making "free men," capable of the enjoyment of rational liberty, has merely increased the number of pagans and savages. Civilization has been forced to fly before barbarism. Such are the results of the philanthropical efforts of the predecessors of our abolitionists!

THE BRITISH WEST INDIES AND BRITISH GUIANA.

It will not be denied by our abolitionists that the British Emancipation act of 1834, by which 663,899 negroes in the British American colonies were manumitted, has proved no blessing, either to the whites or to the negroes. Instead of "being turned from brutes into freemen"—as our philanthropists desire—the blacks have sunk as fast as possible into the former state of their African ancestors. They seem to hasten to embrace destruction; indeed, their only ambition appears to be to get back as speedily as possible to a state of barbarism, and to live, as their forefathers lived in Africa, in dirty villages, surrounded by filth, removed from all responsibility, and passing their lives in ignorance; immorality, and sloth. That that act has been a great failure, even the British themselves, with all their pride and self-esteem, do not deny. All their once splendid colonies are going to decay, and so hopeless are the prospects for the future, that they even talk of withdrawing the white population from some of the islands, leaving them in the undisputed possession of the African race.

Great Britain has shown no little solicitude to ascertain the real state of things in her West India colonies. For this purpose she appointed, in 1842, a select committee, consisting of some of the most prominent members of Parliament, with Lord Stanley at their head. In 1848, another committee was appointed, with Lord George Bentinck as its chairman, to inquire into the condition of the British West India colonies and Mauritius, and to consider whether any measures could be adopted for their relief. The reports of both committees show, beyond all doubt, that unexampled distress existed in the colonies. The report of 1848 declares :

" That many estates in the British West India colonies have
' been already abandoned; that many more are in the course of
' abandonment; and that, from this cause, a very serious diminu-
' tion is to be apprehended in the total amount of production."

A third commission was appointed in 1850, to inquire into the condition and prospects of British Guiana. Lord Stanley, in his report to Mr. Gladstone, the Secretary of the British Colonies, says:

" Of Guiana generally it would be but a melancholy task to dwell
' upon the misery and ruin which so alarming a change must have
' occasioned to the proprietary body; but your commissioners feel
' themselves called upon to notice the effects which this wholesale
' abandonment of property has produced upon the colony at large.
' Where whole districts are fast relapsing into bush, and occasional
' patches of provisions around the huts of village settlers are all
' that remain to tell of once flourishing estates, it is not to be won-
' dered at that the most ordinary marks of civilization are rapidly
' disappearing, and that in many districts of the colony all travel-
' ling communication by land will soon become utterly impracti-
' cable.

" Of the Abary district : 'your commission find that the line of
' road is nearly impassable, and that a long succession of formerly
' cultivated estates presents now a series of pestilent swamps, over-
' run with bush, productive of malignant fevers.'

" Nor are matters much better farther south. Your commission-
' ers find that the public roads and bridges are in such a con-
' dition that a few estates still remaining on the upper west bank
' of Mahaiva creek are completely cut off, save in the very dry
' season; and that with regard to the whole district, unless some-
' thing is done very shortly, travelling by land will entirely cease.
' In such a state of things, it cannot be wondered at that the herds-
' man has a formidable enemy to encounter in the jaguar and other
' beasts of prey, and that the keeping of cattle is attended with
' considerable loss, from the depredations committed by these ani-
' mals.

" It may be worth noticing," continues Lord Stanley, in his extracts from the report of the committee, " that this district, now
' overrun with wild beasts of the forest, *was formerly the very gar-*
' *den of the colony !* The estates touched one another along the
' whole line of the road, leaving no interval of uncleared land."

The commissioners next visit the east bank of the Demerara river, thus described:

"Proceeding up the east bank of the river Demerara, the gen-
' erally prevailing features of ruin and distress are everywhere per-
' ceptible. Roads and bridges, almost impassable, are fearfully
' significant exponents of the condition of the plantations which they
' traverse; and canal No. 3, once covered with plantations, presents
' now a scene of almost total desolation.

"Ascending the river still higher, your commissioners learn that
' the district between Hobaboe creek and 'Stricken Heaven' con-
' tained, in 1829, eight sugar and five coffee and plaintain estates,
' and now there remain but three in sugar, and four partially culti-
' vated with plantains, by petty settlers, while the roads, with one
' or two exceptions, are in a state of utter abandonment. Here, as
' on the opposite bank of the river, hordes of negro squatters have
' located themselves, who avoid all communications with Europeans,
' and have seemingly given themselves up altogether to the rude
' pleasure of a completely savage life."

Describing another portion of the colony, they say of one district:

"Unless a fresh supply of labor be very soon obtained, there is
' every reason to fear that it will become completely abandoned."
"The prostrate condition of this once beautiful part of the coast,"
are the words which begin another paragraph, describing another
tract of the country. Of a third, "the proprietors on this coast
' seem to be keeping up a hopeless struggle against approaching
' ruin." Again. "The once famous Arabian coast, so long the
' boast of the colony, presents now but a mournful picture of de-
' parted prosperity. Here were formerly situated some of the finest
' estates in Guiana, and a large resident body of proprietors lived
' in the district, and freely expended their incomes on the spot
' whence they derived them."

"Berbice," says Lord Stanley, "has fared no better. Its rural
' population (negroes) amounts to eighteen thousand. Of these,
' twelve thousand have withdrawn from their estates, (to which they
' formerly belonged,) and mostly from the neighborhood of the white
' man, to enjoy a savage freedom of ignorance and idleness, beyond
' the reach of example, and sometimes of control. What are the
' districts which together form the country of Berbice? The Cor-
' entyne coast, the Canje creek, east and west banks of the Berbice
' river, and the west coast, where cotton was formerly the chief
' article produced. To each of these, respectively, the following
' passages, quoted in order, reply:
" ' The abandoned plantations on this coast, which, if capital and
' labor could be procured, might easily be made very productive,
' are either wholly deserted, or else appropriated by hordes of squat-
' ters, who, of course, are unable to keep up, at their own expense,

' the public roads and bridges; and, consequently, all communica-
' tion by land between the Corentyne and New Amsterdam is nearly
' at an end. The roads are impassable for horses or carriages,.
' while for foot passengers they are extremely dangerous. The
' number of villages in this deserted region must be upwards of two
' thousand five hundred; and as the country abounds with fish and
' game, the negroes have no difficulty in making a subsistence. In
' fact, the Corentyne coast is fast relapsing into a state of nature.

" ' Canje creek was formerly considered a flourishing district of
' the country, and numbered eighteen sugar and coffee plantations.
' The coffee cultivation has long since been abandoned, and of the
' sugar estates but eight now remain. They are suffering severely
' for the want of labor, and, being supported principally by African
' and coolie immigrants, it is much to be feared, that if the latter
' leave, and claim their return passages to India, a great part of the
' district will become abandoned.'

" Under present circumstances, so gloomy is the condition of
' affairs here, that the two gentlemen whom your commissioners
' have examined with respect to this district, both concur in pre-
' dicting ' its slow but sure approximation to the condition in which
' civilized man first found it.'

" The negroes, who in a state of, slavery were comfortable and
' prosperous beyond any peasantry in the world, and rapidly ap-
' proaching the condition of the most opulent serfs of Europe, have
' been, *by the act of emancipation, irretrievably consigned to a state*
' *of barbarism !* "

Thus speak the English commissioners. Surely it is no wonder
that the hurrahing of the English people has ceased. The London
Times, for December 1, 1852, says:

" At the present moment, if there is one thing in the world that
' the British public do not like to talk about, or *even to think about,*
' it is the condition of the race for whom that great effort was
' made ! "

And yet, notwithstanding all these trist experiences, our abolitionists
move heaven and earth to reduce this country to a similar unfortunate state. They still keep up the annual celebration of that great
event—the British act of emancipation—by which, in the language
of one of their number, more than half a million of human beings
were " *turned from brutes into free men!* " as if not exactly the
contrary had taken place! Emancipation has been a total, a
wretched failure; and it has illustrated a singular feature of the
negro race, namely: that just as there are certain grains and fruits
which the industry of man has redeemed by careful culture from-
their original and savage nature—from some wild grass or bitter
nut, which, if withdrawn from his care, will relapse back to their
original type—just so does the African in these colonies, when left
to himself, relapse back, stage by stage, to the original barbarism
of his fathers.

It will hardly be necessary to speak of Jamaica, that once flourishing and progressive island. Our papers, our public men, have too often described, in glowing colors, the downfall of its commerce, agriculture, and general happiness. But I have nowhere seen the true condition: of the island, under the operation of the British system of free labor for the production of tropical products, better illustrated than from the official reports from the island itself. It is scarcely credible that such a picture as the following should have been issued by a report of the central board of health of Jamaica, in the year 1852:

"Yards" * * * "which, after a rain, send forth streams
' of the most horrible description; numbers of dilapidated and fall-
' ing houses, useless for all habitable purpose; ruined walls and
' remnants of fences, together with unenclosed sites of pulled-down
' houses, covered with filth and brush, complete the scene of every
' old Jamaica township, and the outskirts of the new.

"In villages, and in small settlements, the huts or dwellings of
' the negroes are composed chiefly of mud walls, sometimes of
' wattles plastered with the same." * * *
  * * * "In very few cases are they raised off the ground, nor
' are they floored in any way." * * * "Ventilation, or the
' admission of fresh air, is almost invariably neglected.

"These small, dark, unventilated houses are frequently over-
' crowded, especially at night; within the small space of a few
' square feet, perhaps on the bare ground, or may be on a mattress
' or mat, or in some cases on a bed, with a whole family of eight
' or nine persons, of all ages and of both sexes, huddled together,
' with the door and so-called window closed; all clad in the same
' clothes which they wore through the day, with children sleeping
' on mattresses, often soaked and half rotten with urine and other
' secretions. Should there accidentally be a hole or crevice, this is
' immediately closed up by means of rags or something of that kind.
' The rush of odors on opening such a place must be experienced to
' be understood."

"As regards water for domestic purposes, it is very much to be
' feared that a large portion of our poor population seldom think of
' that. Their persons are never abluted, save in crossing a river,
' or being exposed to a heavy shower of rain.

"Among the lower classes, the majority, not being compelled by
' circumstances to be field laborers, are too lazy to move; they
' frequently squat down all day in a sort of sullen apathy; they eat
' and drink and sleep like the brute that perisheth; but all the
' more active impulses of their human nature appear to be as little
' excited as if they were totally wanting.

"It is a well-known fact, that all the towns and villages contain
' a large number of negroes, who have no ostensible means of earn-
' ing their livelihood; the way in which they subsist is an enigma

' to themselves and others. Exposure in the night air is very
' prevalent among the lower classes; under various excuses, they
' meet in numbers, frequently in the open air, or under temporary
' sheds, or at the performance of wakes over the dead, and also at
' their revels at john-canoeing, as it is termed, about Christmas
' time; on these or other occasions of that kind, they give full scope
' to animal enjoyment; and at the pitch of the excitement of the
' prevailing passions, their gestures and acts resemble more those of
' demons than of human beings."

No wonder that cholera, under such circumstances, is literally
the scavenger disease. More than any other disease, it seeks the
haunts of filth and vice, and there slays its thousands. How fearfully must its ravages be increased, when not combated by medical aid, nor sufficient sanitary police measures. In Jamaica, Mr.
Buxton estimates that during the late visit of this disease and the
small pox, 40,000 persons perished! This would be fully equivalent to a decimation of the population, as the same, according to
Governor Barkly's estimate, is composed of—

Blacks - - - - - - - -	293,128
Colored - - - - - - -	68,529
White - - - - - - - -	15,776
Total - - - - - -	377,433

But it must not be supposed that Jamaica is an exaggerated case.
In Barbados, according to Dr. Thomas, out of a population of
140,000 souls, 135,000 were more or less affected; 50,000 had
cholera in its developed form; and of these, 18,000, or *thirty-six
per cent.*, *died*, making a little more than one-seventh of the whole
population of the Island. In St. Kitts, according to Dr. Cooper,
3,920 perished, out of a population of 24,571, being nearly one-
sixth of the whole population. Antigua is perhaps better provided
with medical attendance than the majority of the British West India
Islands, and yet we find, in a Parliamentary paper, that out of a
population of 31,000 souls, not more than 8,056 are provided with
regular medical aid.

Such are thy triumphs, philanthropy! Such are the blessings
which the unhappy negro race has received from the British emancipation act. Civilization and humanity shudder. Barbarism, in
its coarsest attributes, has gained a strong foothold also in this continent. Large sums are annually collected in the United States,
for the purpose of publishing and circulating incendiary tracts, tending to reduce 4,000,000 more helpless beings to even a worse state
than just depicted. It would be better, and more christianlike,
too, to devote those sums to the medical relief and moral instruction
of the injured race in Jamaica and other British Islands.

English authors and statesmen still continued to speak encour-
agingly of the colonies, to profess confidence in eventual results,

until the testimony collected by the House of Commons committee, in 1853, put an end to all possibility of denial, and the ruin of the colony is finally admitted to be complete and hopeless.

A single extract from the testimony must suffice. Captain Hamilton, of the royal navy, in the course of his evidence, had declared that the Island of Jamaica was a desert. Here follows his examination by the members of the committee:

"*Chairman.* You made use of a phrase, some time ago, with re-
' spect to Jamaica having become a desert. Will you explain to what
' extent you apply that term?

"*Captain Hamilton.* I mean that, in going to plantation estab-
' lishments that had evidently been once splendid buildings, where
' there had been a great outlay of capital on a grand scale, you find
' the roofs tumbling in, the places deserted, nobody in them, grass
' growing in the rooms, and perhaps rats and snakes in those very
' rooms, and a deserted, melancholy appearance, that certainly goes
' to one's heart to view.

"*Chairman.* Is that applicable to only one part, or is it the gen-
' eral character?

"*Captain Hamilton.* It is the general character.

"*Mr. Bright.* That is not the case in Jamaica, but in those par-
' ticular locations?

"*Captain Hamilton.* No; the general character of Jamaica is,
' that it gives you the impression of a place going to decay. Speak-
' ing of the population of Jamaica, I do not refer to the capitalist
' planters of old times, but to the present population of Jamaica, and
' their locations and cultivations.

"*Mr. Bright.* Do you think the term '.desert' was quite appli-
' cable to the state of things there?

"*Captain Hamilton.* I should say peculiarly applicable, without
' any exaggeration."

The effect produced upon the British mind by evidences such as this, may be best gathered by an extract from Lord Palmerston's organ, the London *Morning Herald*, of the 8th September, 1855:

" We have of late, as occasion served, directed the attention of
' our readers to the condition of the most valuable of our West In-
' dian possessions, and have endeavored to trace to its true source,
' in a vicious and mistaken policy, the ruin which not only impends,
' but has actually fallen, upon those Islands, *once the boast and*
' *glory* of the British Crown, now the by-word of the commercial
' nations of the earth. Jamaica, by nature the richest of these de-
' pendencies, is reduced to a state of collapse, from which recovery
' seems to be hopeless. Efforts have been made to stimulate once
' more her industry, to raise her crushed proprietary, and to give
' them once again opportunity and hope. So far, those efforts have
' not been successful. In the recent advices, we can perceive no
' symptoms of amendment; on the contrary, the downward tendency

' of affairs continues, as if, for the unhappy Jamaicans, there is a
' ' lower deep ' yet yawning, which, ' threatening, opens to devour,'
' and from whose frightful vortex there seems to be no hope of es-
' cape." * * *

" Although the ruin of Jamaica has been more rapid and irresist-
' ible than any of the other Islands, desolation rests upon the entire
' archipelagus, and sooner or later will involve them all."

But the French Islands, Martinique and Guadaloupe, are in no
better condition. The beautiful towns, dwellings, and public works,
formerly existing there under the French dominion, are now in ruins,
while the colored population throng the streets in idle mirth, and
sleep in the mid-day sun, with wooden blocks to serve as pillows
to their heads. It is wholly unnecessary to give a detailed description; the condition of these Islands is the same as in the British
colonies.

HOW THE BRITISH AND FRENCH REMEDY THE EVIL—AFRICAN AND ASIATIC SLAVE TRADE IN A NEW FORM.

An official report from a district in British Guiana, fifteen years
ago, contains, after having demonstrated the utter impossibility that
the emancipated negroes will work, the following conclusion: "; Un-
' less a fresh supply of labor be very soon obtained, there is every
' reason to fear that the district will become completely aban-
' doned." The philanthropical British Government, in order to
save the colonies from the approaching destruction, resolved to remedy the evil by taking recourse to a new species of slave trade. It
introduced persons bound to service under the name of apprentices,
or coolies, or colonists, from Africa, the East Indies, and China.
An agent, a Mr. Scott, was appointed for that purpose by the British Government, in China. The emigrants, as they are called, have
to undergo an examination by a medical inspector, who accepts only
such as are in the vigor of life, free from disease, healthy, well-
formed, and able. They must be agriculturists, acclimated to the
tropics, accustomed to hard labor and exposure, and specially
versed in the culture of sugar, cotton, and rice. They belong to a
class which may be said to be exhaustless, since there are fifty millions of people in the Liang Kwang district alone, and nearly as
many in each viceroyalty of the empire. The terms for which they
engage are at least five years, but generally ten years; the total
cost of the Chinese laborer is estimated at $80 per annum, which is
far below the cost of slave labor, independent of the risk which the
planter runs in his original investment.

But how horrible is this traffic! The African slave trade was
nothing compared with it. Thousands of unfortunate beings find
their destruction on the ocean. The British Parliamentary reports

of 1857–'58 state that, "according to a return recently sent home
' by the British Minister at Washington, the number of coolies
' which had embarked in British ships for Cuba was 10,791, of
' which, however, no less than 1,586, or 14¾ per cent., died on the
' voyage. Of 373 embarked in the British ship 'Admiral,' 90, or
' more than 24 per cent., died on the voyage. The 'Waverley,' an
' American vessel, bound from Swatao (an illegal port) to Callao,
' with 450 Chinese coolies on board, landed at Manilla, having lost
' the captain. The Chinamen, believing that they had arrived at
' their port of destination, wished to go on shore, and attempted to
' take possession of the boats in order to do so. The captain, to
' prevent them, fired into them, and the crew, fearing a revolt,
' armed themselves, and the Chinamen were, after a short struggle,
' driven below, and the hatches closed up; and opening them some
' twelve or fourteen hours afterwards, it was found that nearly three
' hundred of the unfortunate beings had perished by suffocation."

The British report adds: "That such results are shocking to
' humanity, and disgraceful to the manner in which the traffic is
' carried on, there can be no question."

But, in spite of all these enormities, the British Government continues the trade, to amend the error it has committed by emanci-
pating the negro slaves in its colonies. A terrible improvement,
indeed!

The French screw propellor "Charles Martel" arrived from
Swatao, China, on the 6th February, 1860, at Havana, with a car-
go of Chinese coolies. She took on board nine hundred and sixteen
of them. Of these, five hundred and sixteen died on the passage,
and seven after the vessel had been in the harbor for two days, leaving, out of nine hundred and sixteen souls, only three hundred and
ninety-three! If the vessel had sailed as far as to Europe, not a
single survivor would have remained!

It must not be forgotten that the traffic is carried on against the
laws of China. The Government of that country prohibits the
people from emigrating. The people themselves are against it, as
will be seen from the following translation of a Chinese proclamation which I find in a message from the President of the United
States, communicating information in regard to the slave and coolie
trade, of May 19, 1856. Well may the Chinese, in this instance,
style the civilized nations engaged in the traffic, barbarians! Must
the latter not feel ashamed at the rebuke they receive at the hands
of that semi-civilized people?

"PROCLAMATION ISSUED BY THE SCHOLARS AND MERCHANTS OF AMOY.

" *Notice, being an exposure of, for the purpose of counteracting, the artifices of hardened
miscreants who impose on the people and seduce them to their destruction.*

"From the time that the barbarians began to trade at Amoy,
' they have had the practice of buying people to sell again; sub-
' jecting those guiltless of crime to cruel treatment, and employing

' evil-disposed and traitorous natives to entice away peaceable
' people. These agents, styled brokers, consisting of some scores
' intimately leagued together, would attach to themselves several
' hundreds of others, and, removing all restraint from their inordi-
' nate cupidity, would follow the course of their interest wherever it
' might lead, without any scruple. They have daily in the country,
' along the coast, sought about in all directions for persons whom
' they might entice away, with the end of making gain for them-
' selves by the detriment of others. By the prospect of minute
' advantage, they drew away lonely and destitute persons, while they
' held out alluring baits to seduce the younger members of settled
' families. Their tricks were innumerable, and they would dex-
' terously conceal their real designs. They would pretend to hire
' their victims for employment by which they might realize a liveli-
' hood, and then drive them into the pits prepared ; or they would
' cheat them with promises of advantage, (here some Malay words
' are used which are unintelligible,) and thus get them within their
' power ; or perhaps would invite them to travel and divert them-
' selves, and so urge men to destruction. Every kind of abomina-
' tion they were addicted to. The ignorant country people have
' many times thus been lost in numbers. From souls so abandoned
' to covetousness, every spark of innate right feeling must have de-
' parted.

" The men, being inveigled to barbarian houses and ships, are
' publicly sold. When once amongst them, they cannot understand
' their gibberish, and they are kept in close confinement. They
' may implore Heaven, and their tears may wet the earth; but their
' complaints are uttered in vain. When carried to the barbarian
' regions, day and night they are impelled to labor, without intervals
' even for sleep. To advance or retreat is equally impossible to
' them ; death is their sole relief.

" Moreover, they can transmit or receive no intelligence ; none
' knows whether they be alive or dead, and the hearts of their pa-
' rents and families are torn with anxiety. The succession of their
' families is cut off—an injury for which nothing can atone. Alas !
' those who, living, were denizens of the central flowery country,
' dead, their ghosts wander in strange lands. O, azure heaven
' above ! in this way are destroyed our righteous people !

" Our present suggestion is, that the benevolent and respectable
' public shall unite in exercising their influence to repress these
' practices. Let fathers caution their sons, and elder brothers their
' younger brothers, for seeing the evil, and guarding against it: Let
' none misguidedly lend themselves to promote the schemes of wicked
' traitors. Let us mutually warn each other, and point out to all
' men the roads which, if life to one, are of death to ten thousand.
' We venture, as above, to express our humble but sincere and

4

' heartfelt sentiments, trusting that they may receive the considera-
' tion of the public.

"Notification by the scholars and merchants of Amoy.

"A true translation: M. C. MORRISON."

"Can the following facts be tolerated?

"Man, being born of heaven and earth, who is without a father
' and a mother, and who is not either a man or a woman, and how
' can they be deceived by men, and fall into their snares?

"Now, I saw in the port of Macao innumerable persons engaged
' in the traffic of buying and selling Chinese; and I know this to
' be the fact from personal knowledge and observation.

"There are already in existence five places, vulgarly called
' 'Chutsze Kwan,' or 'Pig-pens;' one at Hwa Wang Kee, one at
' Puh Ma Hong, one at Hia Wan Kee, one at San Tsing Lou,
' under the sign of Tsung Kai Kee; but the one that has the most
' men is at Sha Lan Tsze.

"Each barracoon procures its men from swindlers, who obtain
' them through deception. The price they pay for each head is eight
' dollars. They frequently purchase and keep them in readiness,
' so that one of these barracoons may have several tens of men, and
' another several hundreds. They wait to embark together, and all
' are shipped to foreign countries, where they are resold for perhaps
' over a hundred dollars per head.

"After their persons are thus sold, they then turn the bodies of
' the Chinese into fish-baits, by which Bêche de Mer is obtained, or
' make use of their persons as beasts of burden, in which capacity
' they undergo all the hardships incident to the clearing of wild
' lands, or else they place their persons in the brunt of an engage-
' ment, where they have to brave the hazards of the cannon. Be-
' sides, there are other unknown evils in their becoming slaves to
' foreigners, and their being used by them at their own will—evils,
' too, of many forms.

"But how are these men seduced? Plainly, because at the out-
' set they are often taken in by swindlers, who would address them
' as follows:

"'I have a relation, who keeps a carpenter's shop at Macao; he
' is desirous of employing a cook. By my recommending you to
' his shop, you will receive in the first year a few moce per month
' for your wages. Your apprenticeship will expire at the end of
' three years; in that case, your monthly wages will be four dollars.'
' Upon seeing a neat and slender fellow, he would say, 'I should
' like to recommend you to a foreign house, as a servant.' Meet-
' ing with the stout and strong, he would say, 'There are men who
' would furnish you with a capital, and I should like to go with you to
' California.'

"Finding his victim wealthy, talented, and young, he would ac-

' cost him, and say, ' I should like to accompany you to see the
' sights, and take you with me to a refreshment room.'

"Thus he watches opportunities and adapts himself to circum-
' stances, employing, moreover, numerous plans and schemes, which
' cannot be discovered and stated, to seduce his victims. When
' once the simpletons credit his fair speeches, they are then forthwith
' accompanied by him through Tih Hing Kee (Howqua's street) in
' Canton, where they step on board a Macao fast boat, that serves
' as a jail for criminals.

"On the next day they are hurried down to Macao, where, upon
' landing, they repair to the barracoons; there they are taught what
' to say; and as they pass muster or examination, they are not per-
' mitted to cry aloud. If any foreigner should question them, each
' is obliged to say that he is poor, and cannot see his way to obtain
' a livelihood, and that he takes pleasure in selling his person. But
' if any should disobey these instructions, the scolding and the lash
' would inevitably be increased.

"Though some who reached this hell of earth against their own
' inclinations, yet they could not help it; for this reason, some un-
' dertook to escape by climbing over walls, but were recaptured by
' foreign devils, and were accordingly flogged to death before the
' rest as a warning. In one of these barracoons, some have even
' gone so far as to commit suicide by hanging themselves. I have
' known of ten such cases.

"But some of those who perished deserve pity; others do not.
' Those who do not, were the rebels found among them. Since
' we could not decapitate them for their crime, still we may thank
' their enemies for having put an end to them. But those who
' deserve pity were some virtuous private citizens found among them,
' who never could return to serve their parents, and were hopeless
' as regards supporting their wives and children. If I still desire
' to harbor and suppress such facts as these, how can I face heaven
' and earth?

"Therefore, whenever an individual is missing, first let a notice
' be issued, and search be made at different places; then one ought
' to repair immediately to the barracoons at Macao, and solicit a
' foreigner to make an inquiry of the superintendent of the ' pigs,'
' as to which of the barracoons the missing person was sold. He
' assuredly can be seen, and his whereabouts known. The superin-
' tendent of the ' pigs' will, of course, demand the sum of five
' dollars for the passage and board, before he would allow the per-
' son to be redeemed. Should he be dissatisfied with this sum, one
' ought then, by all means, to go to the Senate of Macao for con-
' sultation. The foreign magistrate will undoubtedly decide the
' matter according to equity; he takes no fee for it; he is able to
' deliver the person back, but if the man had passed over to the
' hands of foreigners, it would be difficult to recover him.' I have

' experienced all these things myself; there is nothing empty in
' what I say.

" If every parent and friend should circulate this matter far and
' wide, and admonish the wealthy, the talented, the sons, and the
' nephews, who live in the neighboring villages, to be particularly
' on their guard; if, in like manner, the poor, who hire themselves
' out as domestic servants, together with motherless children, should
' be treated with greater compassion, and be made fully acquainted
' with my advice; should these things be done, till we see that both
' those who are of age should escape the danger that besets them,
' and those who are under age would not hear deception, then this
' anonymous effort of mine will be of infinite service.

" Respectfully submitted by the Youth's Assistant, and one who
' cannot endure these facts.   CANTON.

" N. B.—This paper was first published in Canton, in October,
' 1855, and recently a second edition of 3,000 copies has been cir-
' culated.   TRANSLATOR."

The American Minister, Peter Parker, issued, on the 10th of
January, 1856, the following proclamation:

" *Public Notification.*—The undersigned, Commissioner and Min-
' ister Plenipotentiary of the United States of America to China, in
' accordance with instructions of his Government, in relation to the
' so-called coolie trade, ' publicly to discountenance the same on his
' arrival in China,' issues this public notification to all whom it may
' concern:

" Whereas the history of the traffic in Chinese coolies, as carried
' on in vessels of the United States, and under other flags, during the
' past few years, is replete with illegalities, immoralities, and re-
' volting and inhuman atrocities, strongly resembling those of the
' African slave trade in former years, some of them exceeding the
' horrors of the ' middle passage '—women and children having been
' bought for the purpose, and others not merely seduced under false
' pretences, ignorant of their destination, but some forcibly abducted,
' and violently borne to countries unknown to them, never to return;
' and not only by the ancient statutes of the Chinese empire, but by
' recent proclamation, the Imperial Government has prohibited the
' same, threatening with death the ' brokers, hardened miscreants,
' who impose upon the people, and seduce them to their destruc-
' tion;' and whereas the correspondence of the Imperial Govern-
' ment with this legation has evinced its strong disapproval of the
' traffic, describing it in terms which place it upon a level with the
' slave trade itself; and, admitting the trade proper *per se*, it has
' been carried on in localities where *foreign trade is not permitted*
' *by any treaty, and is therefore illegal;* and the foreign name has
' been rendered odious by this traffic, hundreds and thousands of
lives having been inhumanly sacrificed, not perhaps intentionally,

'but nevertheless they have been sacrificed, and, in some instances,
'in a manner than which nothing more revolting can be conceived,
'whilst others who have survived have scarcely been more fortu-
'nate; and whereas the amicable relations of the two Governments
'are being jeopardized, and honorable and lawful commerce imper-
'illed, and even the lives of those engaged in the inhuman pursuit
'have been exposed to the vengeance of those whose relations or
'friends have been bought, kidnapped, or grossly deceived, in the
'progress of the coolie trade; the undersigned, therefore, calls upon
'all citizens of the United States to desist from this irregular and
'immoral traffic, and makes known, to all whom it may concern, the
'high disapprobation thereof of the Government of the United States,
'and forewarns all who may hereafter engage therein that they will
'not only forfeit the protection of their Government while so doing,
'in whatever consequences they may be involved, but, furthermore,
'render themselves liable to the heavy penalties to which the traffic,
'if as hitherto in some instances conducted, may expose them.

"This notification respects the 'coolie trade,' in contradistinc-
'tion to voluntary emigration of Chinese adventurers; between
'these, there exists a wide difference.

"Regulations for the business of furnishing Chinese labor to coun-
'tries that may desire the same, and for affording facilities to Chi-
'nese voluntarily disposed to render such service, in providing out-
'fit and passage, and means and freedom of return at their option,
'may be subject of future treaty stipulation or Government arrange-
'ment on the part of Western nations and China.

"The United States consuls will be instructed to convey copies
'of this notification to the proper Chinese authorities at the five
'ports.

"Given under my hand and seal of office, this 10th day of Janu-
'ary, 1856.

[L. S.]　　　　　　　　　　"PETER PARKER."

But what is the condition of those coolies who have survived the
terrors of the sea, and the ill-treatment at the hands of unmerciful,
money-making sea captains, when they have arrived at the place of
their destination?　Let our Northern fanatics and mistaken philanthropists read the following:

The number of Asiatic and African laborers imported into the
British West Indies during the years 1848 to 1857 amount to
53,001; of which, 6,543 are from Sierra Leone, 6,866 from St.
Helena, 24,520 from the East Indies, and 2,107 from China.　Into
Mauritius, during the same time, were imported 106,279; of which,
105,283 were from the East Indies.　The total number imported
into this island, from 1843 to 1857, is no less than 186,984.

Out of four thousand five hundred coolies imported into Jamaica
in 1846 and 1847, *only one-half remained alive in* 1851, and these

were wandering about, half naked and half starved, living in wayside ditches and dens in the towns, infecting the negroes with their idleness, profligacy, and paganism.

From 1847 to 23d March, 1858, 28,777 coolies shipped for Cuba. Of these, more than 4,000 died on the passage. Of those that arrive, I am assured by a recent traveller that the annual deaths are at least ten per cent.; to use his own words, "*they are considered as raw material to be worked up into sugar.*" If we reflect that the engagements are for ten years; that of their miserable pay of four dollars per month, one-half is retained under the terms of their contract, *to be paid at the conclusion of their engagement— id est*, at the end of the ten years—the truth of this horrible statement, that they are "worked up as raw material," becomes apparent, and its motive equally obvious. *The coolie must not be alive at the end of ten years;* there would be due him $240; and a new one, a fresh worker, could be bought for $100, instead of the miserable Asiatic, worn-out, decrepit, dying, valueless as "raw material!"

Oh, you Christian, philanthropical anti-slavery men of Exeter Hall, who constantly bewail the fate of our well-clad, well-fed, and contented negroes! Why do you not turn your attention to these cruelties, protected and carried on by your own British Government? Extend your humanitarian feelings merely over the slaves in the United States! Where is your Duchess of Sutherland? Where your aristocracy which abhors slavery "so much?"

But now a word about the African *apprentices.*

This new form of slave trade was first devised by England. In 1851, authority was sent from the Colonial Office to the Governor of Sierra Leone, to send out colonists, as they were termed, to the West Indies. A contract was made with an English firm—Hythe, Hodge, & Co.—by the British Government, for the exportation of a large number of these colonists. Thirty-five to forty thousand were actually exported. How were they obtained? The first thing heard of them was a proclamation by Governor Roberts, of Liberia, stating that the contractors were *buying up their colonists* at ten dollars a head, being nearly the same price that slaves were bought for under the old regimé of the slave trade. A writer in the Westminster Review admits that the *colonists* were *bought*, and that none could be obtained voluntarily:

"Why not, then, import free immigrants from Africa? Poor, mis-
' erable heathen! What a good thing it would be to convert them to
' Christianity, always supposing that they did not first convert back
' the creoles to Fetichism; and then you might get any number of
' them, and fill the labor market as full as you pleased!" (And
make money in the bargain, you sanctimonious hypocrites!) "There
' was only one objection to this plan; and that was, that though

'Africans might be *bought to any amount*, yet, when free, they
'would not come!"

Great Britain was absolutely shamed into abandoning this scheme
to procure a sufficient supply of labor for her colonies, after thirty-
five or forty thousand miserable Africans had been bought and sold
into slavery under her flag. It is a known fact that she maintains
a large fleet on the coast of Africa, year after year, 'to capture
slavers. But what becomes of the negroes thus taken and liberated?
The Parliamentary report for 1857–'58 sheds some light on this
subject:

"One or two captures of slavers have taken place (in 1857.)
'The 'Arab' has landed 362 persons in Jamaica. The 'Alecto'
'has landed 410 at St. Helena, of whom a large number died. Of the
'survivors, 150 have been taken to British Guiana in the 'Dominic
'Dale,' and the 'Hopewell' has been chartered for the conveyance
'of the rest. No more liberated Africans will be taken to St.
'Helena; and we have entered into arrangements for the prompt
'conveyance to the West Indies of any who may be carried into
Sierra Leone."

The British, the allies of our abolitionists, call that "liberating."
Instead of carrying the negroes back, whence they were taken, they
transport them to the West Indies, as "apprentices!"

France was not slow to profit by the example given by Great
Britain. Her colonies, too, are perishing, and crying out, that
without compulsory labor they must languish, and languishing,
must die. So the French, after bestowing freedom in their colonies
on those who were born slaves, are now making compensation for
their error by enslaving men who were born free. In spite of the
outcry of the civilized press, slaves, by tens of thousands, are now
being poured annually by the French Emperor into his colonies; he
has set on foot an "emigration" from South Africa to the West Indies, conducted by the firm of Messrs. Régis at Marseilles. In 1857,
the ships "Clara" and "Orion" landed in Martinique 701, and
the "Stella" 625 persons at Guadaloupe. The unhappy victims
rise on their oppressors, and the journals of the day are filled with
accounts of captains and crews attacked by their coolie or African
apprentices. The Emperor, with high-handed violence, abuses the
weakness of Portugal, because she interferes to prevent the slave
trade in her own colonies; and the last news from the French
Antilles is, that in addition to the 12,000 coolies and Africans imported into Martinique and Guadaloupe for 1853, provision has
recently been made for 18,000 more of the "raw material," to wit,
7,000 Africans under the Régis contract, and 11,000 coolies.

Senator Seward, the great anti-slavery apostle, has recently
returned from a tour in the Old World. He was most cordially
received by the Emperor and Empress of France, with whom he
had a private interview—most likely, for the purpose of consulting

how to destroy this Union, the thorn in the eyes of all despots. To the Queen of England he is stated to have said, that he *came to Europe to study despotism.* I wonder if he has also studied the coolie and apprentice trade. Napoleon, at least, might have been able to give him some "reliable" facts on that subject.]

The contract of these unfortunate wretches—I mean the African apprentices—is published in the papers of the day, and is justly characterized as a receipt for killing the greatest number of laborers in the shortest time. The wages are about *nine cents* a day for men, *four* for women, and *two* for children, up to the age of fourteen years; out of which they are to pay for their own clothing, and expense of their own sickness, and a reservation of *ten per cent. monthly* is to be made for the expenses of returning home at the end of the contract. Compare the condition of these "free" laborers with the well-fed, well-lodged, well-clothed, and carefully-tended laborers of the South, and say, in the name of a common humanity, which of these two systems is preferable.*

SLAVERY IN THE UNITED STATES.

There hardly can be one man found, if he is honest and sincere in his pretensions, and if he has read with care the preceding chapters of this work, who will not concede that negro slavery, as it exists in the United States, is infinitely superior to any condition, physically and morally, under which the African race is living elsewhere, either in a state of freedom or slavery. The writer does not profess to be a lover of slavery in any form. He would rather see the negro free, if the enjoyment of his freedom would not be attended with worse consequences to both whites and blacks than his present condition at the South. But history, that grave and incorruptible judge of human affairs, shows too clearly that the negro is incapable of taking care of himself; that he must be cared for, if he is to emerge out of his African barbarism, or to be prevented from relapsing into it. His race is marked with peculiarities which render it totally unable to assume or maintain any national character. In their native land, where these negroes enjoy freedom in its widest sense, they have never emerged from barbarism. If the power to wield our own physical and political strength is freedom, if the absence of any force or restraint is the highest gift to man, then why have not these negroes, with such privileges, become a great nation? Why is it that in St. Domingo, the British and

* Mr. Frank Blair boasted, a short time ago, in a speech made at New York, that, in spite of the declamations of Democrats, as to the bad results of emancipation, the British colonies were in a prospering condition. If that is so, it must be ascribed to the importation of coolies, but not to the emancipation of the slaves.

French colonies, they have not advanced in civilization, after they became free? Why is it that they have relapsed into an uncivilized, savage state? Why is it that in the Northern States, in the midst of the Sewards, the Greeleys, Sumners, Garrisons, Phillipses, and other political quasi-philanthropists, they do not occupy a higher position; that the most civilized of them do not aspire above the positions of barbers, waiters, and whitewashers? That wherever they live in groups together in our cities, they have in general adopted the lowest grades of pursuits, and seem to live in contented subservience to the white population?

What is freedom, which is sounded from the tribunes of demagogues, and the pulpits of fanatic, hypocritical preachers? It is no more and no less than a system of wise and universal restraint, so that no man may use his natural rights, irrespective of the rights of others. It is the system of nature itself. Order is Heaven's first law. By this the planets are governed, and limits and spheres, and attraction and gravitation, and the other great arrangements and forces of nature, remain undisturbed. It is this principle of personal restraint which lies at the foundation of all good laws, which regulates the relations and subordinations of child and parent, servant and master, the soldier and the chief, ward and guardian, and maintains the position that things innocent in themselves shall not be permitted when they lead to the injury of others. This, alone, is freedom, and the freedom of civilization; it is the freedom of checks and balances, and is worthless in any other form.

The slavery which we see in the Southern States is precisely the result of the necessity of restraint upon a class too ignorant to exercise self-control, brought into this condition by a foreign Power, and against the wishes of the colonists—upon a class which has increased in numbers from the very fact that they are well fed and clothed. Whilst the number of blacks, slave or free, in the United States, is now *twelve-fold the number imported from Africa*, there does not now exist, in the West India Islands, *one-fourth of the number actually imported into those colonies*. The actual miseries of life, such as want of food, of fuel, of employment, against which industry and perseverance are continually called to struggle, and which make so many millions of men unhappy and desperate, the slaves of this country never know. I consider it almost a sin to entice the negro from his Southern home, where he enjoys all the comforts of life necessary for his happiness, and hurry him up to cold, inhospitable Canada, where he finds no friends to take care of him, and where he is subjected to a life of misery and want. It is said that there are now forty-five thousand fugitives in that country, and even our abolitionists will not dare to deny that the former condition of these unfortunate beings, as slaves, was infinitely superior to their present state. In short, the greatest enemy which the negro has, are those pretending friends, the abolitionists of the

North. They would perhaps be less blamable, if they provided for the future welfare and subsistence of the fugitives after they had run them off. But that is not their purpose; to make political capital is all they desire. Is that freedom, to reduce the poor negro to poverty and its consequences—crime and vice—or to place him into a position, where, as in the West Indies, he will be permitted to relapse into the barbarism of his ancestors?

WHAT THE REPUBLICAN PARTY DESIRES.

The tendency of the Republican party, its doctrines and teach-ings, lead directly or indirectly to an abolition of slavery in the Southern States. Governor Seward, the acknowledged leader and the probable candidate for the Presidency in 1860 of that party, openly declared in a speech that there is "an irrepressible conflict" between the free and slave States. The logical meaning of this doctrine is simply that the Republican party will not rest until, by some means or other, slavery has been abolished in the South. Sixty-eight members of Congress, belonging to that party, have signed their names to a recommendation of a book which preaches the abolition of slavery in undisguised terms.* Wendell Phillips, Garrison, and others of that class, also belonging to the Republi-can party, have used even stronger expressions against slavery. Phillips, in a speech made in New York on the 15th of December last, openly declared :

"Well, then, what was Brown's purpose? It was to free slaves. ' Is that an honest act, or not? Is it honest for a slave to rise and ' take his master by the throat, and make his way to liberty *over as* ' *many dead bodies as could lay from Virginia to Canada ?* Is it, ' or is it not? [Several voices. 'No, no.'] Well, I was born at ' the base of Bunker Hill, and I say *it is right.* [Loud and long ' applause, with hisses.] Well, let us pass it. [Cries of 'treason,' ' ' treason,' ' treason,' and disturbance.] I believe, gentlemen and ' ladies, that if a slave, *with the blood of his master on his right* ' *hand*, stood at the door of one of these very men, they would admit ' him, and shut the door behind him against any hound that was ' following him from Virginia to New York."

I recommend to that gentleman, and to those philanthropical and tender-hearted ladies who were present at the said meeting, a peru-sal of the bloody history of negro insurrection of St. Domingo. There they find all their wishes anticipated, and all their prayers fully granted. It must be very amusing and gratifying to their delicate,

* Harrison G. Blake, Republican member of Congress from Ohio, introduced, in the House, March, 1860, a preamble and resolution to abolish slavery in the United States. Sixty Republican members voted for the same.

humane feelings, to read how that unhappy country was wrapped in flames, and every white person, without distinction of sex or age, was brutally massacred. They will read, probably with an indescribable thrill of pleasure, how all whites, not only the slaveholders, who fell into the hands of the negroes, were put to death; how they tore them with red-hot pincers, sawed them asunder between planks, roasted them by a slow fire, or tore out their eyes with red-hot corkscrews. Oh, these philanthropical ladies! How must their hearts beat, if they read how mothers and daughters, beautiful young ladies, were ravished in the presence of their husbands, fathers, and lovers, ' τ the " black brothers in bondage," and, after having satisfied the brutal appetites of those demons, were slaughtered without mercy! If these philanthropists had been living at that time, they would, according to their own words, have protected those brutes within their own doors, "*with the blood of their masters on their right hands.*" For, like those fanatics who originated the rebellion in Hayti, they would excuse themselves with the plea, " that the commission of a civil crime is not possible in a state of slavery." They would have hugged the perpetrators of such demoniacal acts to their bosoms, for "it is right for them to walk over the dead bodies of the whites from Virginia to Canada." It is not impossible that, amongst those Christian and humane ladies present at that meeting, there were mothers, who had sweet, delicate babies at home. How elated, how " philanthropical," must have been their feelings, when, sitting beside the cradle of their own children, they read that in that revolution the *standard of the negroes was, in one instance, the body of a white infant impaled on a stake!*

Such are the *direct* means by which the Republican party strives to abolish slavery. *Indirectly*, they further their scheme by a constant abuse and misrepresentation of the South. All their papers teem with attacks on the " slavery barons," and the institution of slavery in general. Knowing that the great mass of even their own party are averse to an abolition of slavery, or to a repetition of the scenes of the Hayti revolution, they try to deceive them by pretending " that they are only against the extension of slavery, and that they do not desire to interfere with slavery in the States." They occupy the same ground assumed by the British society, which met at the Old Jewry, in London, before the outbreak of the revolution of St. Domingo. As already shown, the members of that society also " disclaimed all intention of interfering with the ' government and condition of the negroes already in the planta- ' tions; publicly declaring their opinion to be, that a general eman- ' cipation of those people, in their present state of ignorance and ' barbarity, instead of a blessing, would prove to them the source of ' misfortune and misery." They *professed* to have nothing more in view than to obtain an act of the Legislature for prohibiting the further introduction of African slaves into the British colonies.

But although such were their ostensible declarations as a public body, the leading members of the society, in the same moment, held a very different language; and even the society itself pursued a line of conduct directly and immediately repugnant to their own professions. Just exactly so it is with our moderate Republicans—the Seward, Greeley, Phillips, and Garrison school, bearing more resemblance with the French *Amis des Noirs*—they do not intend to interfere with slavery where it already exists, but they cannot open their mouths without attacking it. And they are less to be excused than their British and French predecessors, as the former had not the benefit of experience. Had they known that all their philanthropical efforts would merely tend to increase the number of savage people, extend African barbarism over some of the most beautiful and fertile portions of the globe, to the entire exclusion of the white race, I doubt, very much, whether they would have gone so far as they really have. The raid of John Brown into Virginia is but the necessary consequence of the direct and indirect teachings of the Republicans. His act is the "illegitimate child" of that party, and whether they will recognise it or not matters very little. They have been preaching treason for years; they have been disseminating incendiary documents. Bloodshed and civil war called them into life; and if they are permitted by the American people, they will make the whole country a bleeding Kansas, or a second St. Domingo. Their preachers, instead of teaching the holy sentiment, "love thy neighbor like thyself," are polluting the pulpit, making a mockery of religion, disseminating hatred and discord, and preaching "Sharpe's rifles and bloodshed." Instead of expressing their abhorrence against treasonable acts as committed by John Brown, they canonize him, and place him even above Christ. They would glory, if they could incite slaughter, rapine, and destruction, as occurred in St. Domingo. It is time that the honest, patriotic masses of the North emerge from the lethargy into which they have sunk for the last five years, and save the country from those harpies.

That the professions of the Republican party for the rights of the negro are only selfish and hypocritical, appears from the fact that in Massachusetts, the mother State of Republicanism *par excellence*, they have trampled upon the rights of the white emigrant, placing him far below the negro. In that State, a negro is a voter after a residence of *one* year; whilst a foreigner, no matter how intelligent he may be, must have resided *seven* years in the State, before he can enjoy the same right. These freedom and equality shriekers esteem, therefore, the negro seven times higher than those belonging to their own race! Gov. Seward wanted even to exchange free negroes for white immigrants, because the former are always voting the "right" ticket!

There are two ways by which slavery in the United States can be abolished—either by voluntary emancipation, or by rebellion. Let us examine each one of them separately.

Suppose the Southern States should follow the example set, by Great Britain, and emancipate all their slaves. What is to become of the 4,000,000 of negroes? Will they continue to labor, or will they do just as their brethren have done in the West Indies—*id est*, lead an indolent and vagrant life, and relapse into a state of barbarism? Will their position as "free men" be a better one than it is now? Will they be permitted to enjoy the same political rights as the whites, or will they continue to remain an inferior race, just as they are now in the Northern States? Will four millions of negroes live all the time in peace with eight millions of whites, especially in districts where they outnumber the latter?

These questions will easily be answered by any one who has taken the trouble to examine the history of the African race in America. Emancipation in the Southern States would undoubtedly be accompanied by the same results as in the West Indies. It would even be worse than it is there, as the number in this country is much larger than in the West Indies and other British colonies, where the slaves, at the time of the emancipation, numbered only 663,899, and did not live altogether in one country, but were spread over seventeen different islands and colonies.

The second proposition—to free the negroes by open rebellion—is still more disastrous than the first, as it would most probably end in the total annihilation of the poor negroes. It is true, our Republicans do not expect this result, as they probably would rather see. the whites destroyed, just as it was done in St. Domingo. But they forget that eight millions of whites will never be overcome by four millions of blacks. In St. Domingo, there were in 1790 480,000 negro slaves and 24,000 mulattoes against 38,000 whites, or sixteen colored persons to one white; and yet the blacks only succeeded to drive out the white population after they had lost, either by the sword or by famine, no less than 100,000 men! Suppose now that our fanatics should succeed, as they recently attempted, to stir up a rebellion of the negro slaves against the whites in the Southern States, what would be the consequences? We would see all the horrid scenes, the carnage, and diabolical atrocities, of St. Domingo, repeated. On both sides, acts would be committed which would make humanity shudder. The flourishing and fertile plantations would be consumed by flames; devastation would reign supreme in a country now nourishing and enriching, by its products, millions of people. Our philanthropical ladies of the North, who applauded recently the incendiary harangue of Wendell Phillips, would most probably have the consolation and satisfaction that similar hellish outrages, as described in the history of St. Domingo, had been committed by the negroes on the bodies of their white sisters in the South. *But there would hardly be one negro left to come up to the North,*

" with the blood of his master on his right hand," *to be sheltered*
and protected by Wendell Phillips and consorts. The material
welfare, not only of the South, but of the whole country, would be
totally destroyed. Desolation, ruin, and misery, would reign, instead of prosperity and happiness. In short, it would be such a
dismal and mournful downfall as the world has never seen before.
A kind Providence may protect this country from such a calamity
and misfortune !

THE HELPER BOOK.

The reader will easily perceive, after what I have stated so far,
that it will be almost superfluous to say much about a book which
is calculated to destroy the happiness and prosperity of this country,
and introduce discord, civil war, and bloodshed, into our midst. I
cannot, however, forbear to express my greatest surprise that *sixty-
eight* Congressmen—gentlemen aspiring or pretending to be statesmen, sent to Washington as legislators—should ever have permitted
themselves to recommend a work like that. Still more I am astonished that Gov. Seward, a gentleman of undoubted ability—even
considered, by his friends, as one of our best statesmen—should
have joined in recommending a book, written without the least
regard to national economy, and full of fallacious deductions. I
speak not so much of its revolutionary and anti-slavery character—
a good many and abler works have already been published on that
subject—but what surprises me is the ridiculous, and in some respects even childish, application of statistics, the value of which
ought to be better known by legislators.

The book is not so much directed against the South as against
the free white laborers, mechanics, and merchants, of the North !
It openly advocates that the people of the South shall no longer
buy their necessaries of life in the Northern States ; it ridicules,
vilifies, and abuses, the Southern people, that they have a commercial intercourse with the North ; that they support Northern manufactures by their patronage. The doctrine which it lays down, if
carried out, must necessarily result in the destruction and ruin of
the Northern factories, who are now employing thousands of men
and women for the Southern trade. That Northern representatives,
amongst them Senator Seward, have been recommending such a book,
must not a little astonish their constituents, who are now reaping
the benefits accruing from the Southern trade ! The workmen, the
mechanics, the merchants, of the North, will now see how sincere and
honest those demagogues are in their professions for the welfare of
the *free white laborers !* Let them read the following extract from
the Helper book, page 18 :

" The North is the Mecca of our [the Southern] merchants, and

' to it they must and do make two pilgrimages per annum—one in
' the spring, and one in the fall. All our commercial, mechanical,
' manufactural, and literary supplies, come from there. We want
' Bibles, brooms, buckets, and books, and we go to the North; we
' want pens, ink, paper, wafers, and envelopes, and we go to the
' North; we want shoes, hats, handkerchiefs, umbrellas, and pocket
' knives, and we go to the North; we want toys, primers, school-
' books, fashionable apparel, machinery, medicines, tombstones, and
' a thousand other things, and we go to the North for them all.
' Instead of keeping our money in circulation *at home*, by patroni-
' zing our own mechanics, manufacturers, and laborers, we send it
' all away to the North, and there it remains; it never falls into our
' hands again.

"In one way or another, we are more or less subservient to the
' North every day of our lives. In infancy, we are swaddled in
' Northern muslin; in childhood, we we are humored with Northern
' gewgaws; in youth, we are instructed in Northern books; at the
' age of maturity, we sow our 'wild oats' on Northern soil; in mid-
' dle life, we exhaust our wealth, energies, and talents, in the dis-
' honorable vocation of entailing our dependence on our children and
' on our children's children, and to the neglect of our own interests
' and the interests of those around us, in giving aid and succor to
' every department of Northern power. In the decline of life, we
' remedy our eyesight with Northern spectacles, and support our
' infirmities with Northern canes; in old age, we are drugged with
' Northern physic; and finally, when we die, our inanimate bodies,
' shrouded in Northern cambric, are stretched upon the bier, borne
' to the grave in a Northern carriage, entombed with a Northern
' spade, and memorized with a Northern slab!"

And I may add hereto, for all these *Northern* things we "fork
over" our *Southern* money, by which we sustain the Northern
manufactories, and give bread to thousands of Northern laborers,
mechanics, and merchants! And those Northern Republican representatives, Senator Seward included, who recommended that book,
would have it otherwise! They blame and abuse the Southern
people, that they buy from the North; they ascribe it to slavery,
that the South maintains a commercial intercourse with the North,
that she does not manufacture these things herself, or buys somewhere else. If that is really so, I think the Northern workmen will
be very gratified that Southern slavery causes such beneficial results
to them. And I sincerely hope that they will continue to enjoy
them, notwithstanding the Helper book and its Republican signers.

But read, you Northern laborers, mechanics, and merchants, the
following passages. Judge, for yourselves, whether those hypocritical and selfish Republican leaders are really such warm friends of
your interests and welfare as they pretend to be. Read the following words, directed to the Southern people. They must open your

eyes; there can no longer be any doubt that these fanatics are in
earnest to strike down your prosperity, and ruin you and your families forever. Read those glowing appeals to the Southern people,
to make themselves independent—*i. e.*, to buy no longer from you,
and support the Northern manufactories and other industrial
branches of a civilized life. Read how the slaveholders are abused
and vilified, because they maintain a commercial intercourse with
you, and not with another country; or do not manufacture their
own commodities! It is your destruction, your ruin and misery,
which these philanthropical gentlemen are aiming at. They want to
destroy your independence as freemen, by depriving you of the means
of subsistence, in order to make you white slaves, who have to work
day and night for a pittance hardly sufficient to satisfy the most
necessary wants, and who occasionally may be slaughtered by hundreds, as you have seen recently in pious, Republican Massachusetts—I allude to the catastrophe at the Pemberton Mills—sacrificed at the altar of Mammon! But, hear Helper, page 197:

" Merchants of the South, slaveholders, you are the avaricious
' assassinators of your country! You are the channels through
' which more than one hundred and twenty millions of dollars
' ($120,000,000) are annually drained from the South, and conveyed
' to the North. You are daily engaged in the unmanly and unpa-
' triotic work of impoverishing the land of your birth. You are
' constantly enfeebling our resources, and rendering us more and
' more tributary to distant parts of the nation. *Your conduct is
' reprehensible, base, and criminal.*"

Mark, because they buy from the North!

" Whether Southern merchants ever think of the numerous ways
' in which they contribute to the aggrandizement of the North, while
' at the same time they enervate and dishonor the South, has for
' many years, with us, [Helper, Seward, and the sixty-eight,]
' been a matter of more than ordinary conjecture. If, as it would
' seem, they have never yet thought of the subject, it is certainly
' desirable that they should exercise their minds upon it at once.
' Let them scrutinize the workings of Southern money after it
' passes north of Mason and Dixon's line. Let them consider how
' much they pay to Northern railroads and hotels, how much to
' Northern merchants and shop-keepers, how much to Northern
' shippers and insurers, how much to Northern theatres, news-
' papers, and periodicals. Let them also consider what disposition
' is made of it, after it is lodged in the hands of the North. *Is not
' the greater part of it paid out to Northern manufacturers, mer-
' chants, and laborers*, for the very articles which are purchased at
' the North? And, to the extent that this is done, *are not North-
' ern manufacturers, mechanics, and laborers, directly counte-
' nanced and encouraged*, (!) while, at the same time, Southern
' manufacturers, mechanics, and laborers, are indirectly abased, de-

' pressed, and disabled? It is, however, a matter of impossibility,
' on these small pages, to notice or enumerate all the methods in
' which the money wo deposit in the North is made to operate
' against us. Suffice it to say, that it is circulated and expended
' there, *among all classes of the people*, to the injury and impov-
' erishment of almost every individual in the South."

How do you, Northern people, like the idea that the conduct of
your best customers is "*reprehensible*, BASE, and CRIMINAL" (!)
because they buy from you, and "*countenance and encourage*"
your manufacturers, mechanics, and laborers? A great book, that
Helper book! A very good campaign document for the Republicans! But hear it again! You will find some more astonishing
facts. Speaking of the routine of the daily life of a Southern gentleman, Helper, page 199, says:

" See him rise in the morning from a Northern bed, and clothe
' himself in Northern apparel; see him walk across the floor on a
' Northern carpet, and perform his ablutions out of a Northern ewer
' and basin. See him uncover a box of Northern powders, and
' cleanse his teeth with a Northern brush; see him reflecting his
' physiognomy in a Northern mirror, and arranging his hair with a
' Northern comb. See him dosing himself with the medicaments of
' Northern quacks, and perfuming his handkerchief with Northern
' cologne. See him referring to the time in a Northern watch, and
' glancing at the news in a Northern gazette. See him and his fam-
' ily sitting in Northern chairs, and singing and praying out of
' Northern books. See him at the breakfast table, saying grace
' over a Northern plate, eating with Northern cutlery, and drinking
' from Northern utensils. See him charmed with the melody of a
' Northern piano, or musing over the pages of a Northern novel.
' See him riding to his neighbor's in a Northern carriage, or furrow-
' ing his land with a Northern plough. * * * Perhaps our
' Virginia gentleman is a merchant; if so, see him at his store,
' making an *unpatriotic* use of his time in the miserable traffic of
' Northern gimcracks and haberdashery. His labors, his talents,
' his influence, *are all for the North*, and not for the South." * * *

And those Republicans would have it otherwise! They blame,
abuse, and vilify, the Southern people, because "their labors, talents, and influence, *are all for the North!*" What say the Northern workmen, merchants, and mechanics? What the New England
shoemakers?

" We are constantly buying, and selling, and wearing, and using,
' Northern merchandise, at a double expense to both ourselves and
' our neighbors. If we look at ourselves attentively, we shall find
' that we are all clothed *cap-à-pie* in Northern habiliments. Our
' hats, our caps, our cravats, our coats, our vests, our pants, our
' gloves, our boots, our shoes, our under-garments, all come from
' the North; whence, too, Southern ladies procure all their bonnets,
5

' plumes, and flowers; dresses, shawls, and scarfs; frills, ribbons,
' and ruffles; cuffs, capes, and collars. * * *

"We must learn to take care of our money; WE SHOULD
' WITHHOLD IT FROM THE NORTH, and open avenues for
' its circulation at home." * * *

Here, people of the North, have you the Helper-book doctrine,
recommended by Senator Seward and sixty-eight Republican members of Congress! Ask yourselves whether that book is not more
directed against you than against the South! What is to become
of you, of your families, your manufactories, and industries, if that
pernicious doctrine is to be carried out?

The effects of these destructive anti-Northern sentiments, expressed in the Helper book, are already now visible in the attempts
of commercial non-intercourse with the North, made in some of the
Southern States.* The Southern people being taunted by Seward
and the sixty-eight with an "*unmanly and unnational dependence,
which is so glaring that it cannot fail to be apparent to even the
most careless and superficial observer*," (Helper, page 14,) have
merely threatened to suspend their intercourse with the North, and
that alone has been sufficient to embarrass the Northern manufacturers. How would it be, if the Helper doctrine was carried out to
its fullest extent, if the Southern people would buy somewhere
else—for money will buy anywhere—or if they would manufacture
their own commodities which they now receive from the North? Let
Seward and the sixty-eight statesmen answer this question before
their own constituents. Let them explain that, for the furtherance
of their self-aggrandizement and ambitious schemes, they sacrifice
the dearest interests of their own people; that their constant cry of
"free labor" is merely calculated upon to deceive the unaware,
and to lead them blindfolded to their own destruction. But how
can the free white laborers of the North expect protection from
Gov. Seward, when it is known that his estimation of them went so
far as to make an offer to Gov. Smith, of Virginia, to exchange them
for free negroes! That is the apostle of "free labor!"

But these Republican statesmen do not only incite the Southern

---

* Mr. Seward, in his recent speech, aware of the unfortunate results of his irrepressible-conflict doctrine in the New England States, tried to throw, once more,
sand into the eyes of the Northern people, by terming the Southern States "*capital
States*," and the Northern, "*labor* States." The phraseology is not bad; but what
surface ignorance, or superficial imposition, does this treatment of political economy betray! He is not, however, the shallow thinker, but the consummate politician and demagogue. His purpose was evidently to deceive that class of labor
in the free States which is now depressed, or in open rebellion. Reports come in
of the bankrupt condition of labor, in some of its varieties. The strike of the
thousands of shoemakers in Massachusetts attests the gloomy prospects before
working men in that section. Many branches of industry are suffering, and Mr.
Seward, in his speech, attempts to show the reasons to be this collision between
the "capital States" and "labor States." Will the Northern people be deceived
in such a clumsy manner?

people against the Northern laborers, mechanics, and merchants, but even our farmers are not spared. They abuse the slave States, because—

"Maryland buys annually seven millions of dollars worth of hay 'from the North. * * *

"Even in the most insignificant little villages in the interior of 'the slave States, * * * the *agricultural* products of the 'North, either crude, prepared, pickled, or preserved, are ever to be 'found.

* * * "That the profits arising to the North from the sale 'of provender and provisions to the South, are far greater than those 'arising to the South from the sale of cotton, tobacco, and bread- 'stuffs, to the North."

These philanthropical gentlemen then coolly tell the Southern people in that precious book that, "because they buy with their 'money all those things from the Northern laborers, mechanics, 'merchants, and farmers," they are " *degenerate, and nothing short* '*of the complete abolition of slavery can save the South from fall-* '*ing into the vortex of utter ruin.*" A very "logical, states-manlike" conclusion! Suppose they do abolish slavery, and set the four millions of negroes free, permit them to relapse into indo-lence and barbarism, as it has been the case in the British and French colonies, and for want of laborers let their rich plantations, now producing all the money with which the Northern productions are bought, go to decay! Then, perhaps, the Southern people will no longer be "degenerate," because they buy from the North. That will be entirely out of the question, for I hardly believe that our Northern people would sell *without* money. And money would then be a very scarce article in the South. But, according to Helper's own statement, the North would be the greatest loser, as "the profits arising to the North from the sale of provender and 'provisions alone to the South are far greater than those arising to 'South from the sale of cotton, tobacco, and breadstuffs, to the 'North." Let our Northern people learn from these facts where they are to be led by the Republican party; let them stop the evil, ere it is too late! Let them show, next fall, how they appreciate the efforts of Mr. Seward and his sixty-eight statesmen, to destroy the Northern prosperity and future prospects of happiness. For if the Southern people are "degenerate," because they buy from the North, those of the Northwest and the Pacific are more or less so too; for they also buy from the North, although they are free States.

Mr. Seward and his statesmen then proceed to compare in their book the agricultural products of the slave States with those of the free States. They find that, according to the census of 1850, the 13,434,922 of the free States produced $44,782,636 more of wheat, oats, Indian corn, potatoes, rye, barley, buckwheat, beans and peas, clover and grass seeds, flaxseed, garden and orchard products, than the 9,612,979 inhabitants of the slave States. They might just as logically have compared the exports from New York with those of Philadelphia, and then accused the people of the latter city of being indolent, uncivilised, and "degenerate," because their exports do not . ount to as much as those of New York. Is there anything astoni‚ning that 13,434,922 persons should produce $44,000,000 of those products more than 9,612,979? Or is there any blame to be attached to the 400,000 inhabitants of Philadelphia, because they do not export as much as the 800,000 people of New York? Mr. Seward and his Republican statesmen, however, take no notice of that circumstance; they "pitch into" the Southern people most lustily, as will be seen from the following extract:

" There are few Southerners who will not be astonished at the
' disclosure of these statistical comparisons between the free and the
' slave States. That the astonishment of the more intelligent and
' patriotic non-slaveholders will be mingled with indignation, is no
' more than we anticipate. We confess our own surprise and deep
' chagrin at the result of our investigations. Until we examined
' into the matter, we thought and hoped the South was really ahead
' of the North in *one* particular—that of agriculture," etc.

But enough of that clap-trap! How could it ever be possible that gentlemen, like Mr. Seward and the sixty-eight members of Congress, should have recommended such a nonsense, full of fallacious deductions, calculated to operate upon the unwary and simple-minded? European statisticians and political economists must indeed, if they should read that book, receive a very poor opinion of our legislators, especially if they observe how curiously statistics are applied by them.

But mark, in those articles above mentioned, and which comprise the leading staples of exports of the North, the staple products of the South, as cotton, tobacco, and rice, are not included. To balance them, our ingenious friends have found out " that the annual
' hay crop of the free States is worth considerably more in dollars
' and cents than all the cotton, tobacco, rice, etc., annually pro-
' duced in the fifteen slave States." Even some Republican Congressmen have recently made the same statement in Congress. But let us see how that is. At first, everybody knows that the climate in the South permits the farmers to keep almost the whole year their cattle in the field—something which is impossible in the North, on account of cold and snow. They have, therefore, no necessity to make as much hay as the Northern people. But even suppose that the hay crop, and all the uncut grass on the Western prairies, was on the spot really worth more in dollars and cents than all the cotton, tobacco, and rice, of the South, what then? Does that enrich the country at large? Do we draw by it one single dollar to our shores from a foreign country? No; we do not export one single ton of hay, whilst the exportation of cotton alone brought,

during the year ending the 30th of June last, no less than one hundred and sixty-one millions of dollars, or the value thereof, from foreign countries, into our midst, not to speak of the twenty-one millionsof dollars worth of tobacco exported during the same year.

Such are the fallacies in the Helper book. It will remain a matter of surprise for every honest and patriotic American citizen, that one Senator, and sixty-eight members of Congress could have been found to endorse such deceptive statements as contained in that work. I understand that the Republicans generally are recommending the book as a campaign document. I hope they will continue to do so; especially, see that it comes in the hands of our Northern laborers, mechanics, merchants, and farmers, against whom it incites the Southern feeling, urging the South to non-intercourse with the North—something equivalent to the destruction of the happiness and prosperity of thousands of innocent Northern families. Let that book be widely circulated; *it will do no harm to the Democratic party!*

COMPARATIVE STATISTICS OF THE YEAR ENDING JUNE 30, 1859, AS REPORTED BY THE REGISTER OF THE U. S. TREASURY DEPARTMENT.

The total exportation of domestic produce, for the year 1858–'59, from the United States to foreign countries, amounted to the sum of $335,894,385; of which Great Britain (exclusive of the colonies) received $168,786,252, and France $42,699,999. The exportation of raw cotton reached a value of $161,434,923, of which amount—

Great Britain received	$108,727,000
France	22,437,000
Hamburgh and Bremen	7,321,000
Spain	7,122,000
Russia	5,432,422
Sardinia	2,167,019

The total exportation of tobacco was valued at $21,079,038. Bremen and Hamburg received thereof for $4,078,000. Great Britain for $5,420,000. France for $4,202,000. The total exportation of rice amounted to $2,207,148. We have, therefore, for the year 1858–'59, an exportation of—

Raw cotton to the amount of	$161,434,923
Manufactured cotton of domestic produce	4,477,096
Tobacco	21,074,038
Manufactured tobacco of domestic produce	3,334,401
Rice	2,207,148
Total	196,527,606

for only three Southern staples. The amount of tobacco grown in

non-slaveholding States may be deducted from the amount of Southern tobacco consumed in the United States.

It will not be an over-estimate, if I calculate the other Southern
products exported to foreign countries, great many of which are
shipped from Northern ports, to be of a value of no less than
$24,000,000, which would give to the South a total foreign export-
ation of $220,000,000; leaving to the Northern States—the total
exportation of domestic produce being $335,894,385—a balance of
only $115,894,385 of Northern produce! And yet Mr. Seward,
and the sixty-eight statisticians, will make the Northern people
believe that the South is "degenerate" and bankrupt!

The South imports through her own ports goods to the amount of
$32,943,281; the North, through her ports, to the amount of
$305,824,849. If we deduct the $32,943,281 which the South
imports directly, from the $220,000,000 of her annual exports,
there remains a sum of some $188,000,000 to be accounted for.
Suppose, now, that annually $25,000,000 of cash are received of
that sum for circulation in the South, there still remain, in the
hands of the Northern importers, some $163,000,000, for which
the Southern people receive either foreign goods imported into
Northern ports through Northern men, or domestic products of the
Northern States. That is the money with which the South buys
Northern brooms, buckets, shoes, furniture, machinery, tombstones,
provender, provisions, and other innumerable things of Northern
manufacture and growth.

But, also, our commercial marine receives its main support from
the Southern carrying trade. Of the $186,618,178 of domestic
produce exported from the Southern ports, $141,000,000 were in
American bottom, whilst only $44,000,000 were carried by foreign
vessels.

RECAPITULATION.

Imports and Exports of Domestic Produce in 1858-'59.

The North imports through her ports -	$305,824,849
She exports " " " -	149,276,207
Balance *against* the North - • -	156,548,642
The South imports through her ports -	$32,943,281
She exports " " " -	`186,618,178
Balance *for* the South - - - -	143,674,897

If we deduct from the $156,548,642 of the North, $9,000,000
of raw cotton exported from New York and Boston, which, as
Southern product, cannot be included among Northern exports, it
will be seen at a glance that the two balances correspond almost to
a dollar. Of course, the North could not annually import one

hundred and fifty-six millions of dollars more than she exports, if the South did not buy from her. These figures speak volumes.

However disagreeably it may sound in the ears of our Northern philanthropists, yet it cannot be denied that the whole financial system, not only of the United States, but also of England, is based upon the cultivation and growth of cotton in the United States.

From a paper read by J. T. Danton, Esq., before the British Association at Cheltenham, August, 1856, I extract the following conclusions. The gentleman stated in his introduction that his statements were not intended to support, or to oppose, either slavery in general, or any particular form of it. His whole purpose was to show how far Great Britain, as a nation, is implicated in the pending dispute.

"After mature consideration, I deduce from the materials now ' before me, and which I am about to lay before you, the conclu- ' sions :

"I. *That, in the present state of the commercial relations of* ' *the two countries, the cotton planters of the United States are* ' *interested, to the extent of about two-thirds of their exportable* ' *produce, in the maintenance of the cotton manufacture of the* ' *United Kingdom; and*

"II. *That, reciprocally, the cotton manufacturers of the United* ' *Kingdom, and, through them, the entire population of the king-* ' *dom, are interested, to the extent of four-fifths of the raw mate-* ' *rial of that manufacture, in the existing arrangements for main-* ' *taining the cotton culture of the United States.*

"These conclusions I base on the following propositions :

"1. That cotton must be grown, almost entirely, out of Europe, ' and manufactured chiefly in Europe; and, in Europe, chiefly in ' Great Britain.

"2. That cotton has hitherto been grown, and, *as far as yet ap-* ' *pears*, must continue to be grown, chiefly by slave labor.

"3. That, for the last fifty years, Great Britain, seeking her ' supply of cotton all over the earth, with a preference during the ' greater part of that period for the produce of free labor, has yet ' received, during the whole of that period, and continues to receive, ' all the cotton she imports of the better qualities, and by far the ' greater part of all she imports, in bulk as well as in value, from ' countries in which it is grown by slave labor.

"4. That cotton is grown in the United States exclusively by ' slave labor.

"5. That two-thirds, at least, of the slave population of the ' United States are employed in raising cotton for exportation.

"6. That of the cotton thus raised for exportation, about two- ' thirds in quantity, and more than two-thirds in value, is raised ' expressly for the British market, and is regularly imported into, ' and manufactured in, the United Kingdom ; and

"'7. That of the entire quantity of cotton imported into, and
' manufactured in, the United Kingdom, nearly four-fifths in quan-
' tity, and more than four-fifths in value, is, on an average of years,
' obtained from the United States.

"About eighty per cent. of the British supply of cotton come
' from the United States and Brazil alone, and are clearly the pro-
' duce of slave labor. Very little of the three per cent. obtained
' from the Mediterranean can be set down as probably raised by
' free labor; and nearly the whole of the remaining seventeen per
' cent. come from the East Indies. There is not, and never has
' been, any considerable source of supply for cotton, excepting the
' East Indies, which is not obviously and exclusively maintained by
' slave labor, as the Indian Ryot does not appear to be such as to
' his operations, either as laborer for hire, or as an independent
' cotton grower, the productive advantages we are accustomed to
' associate with our idea of free labor. He seems to be, in point of
' fact, little better than a slave. Besides, the cotton of India does
' not hold a high rank in the European market, in point of quality.
' Mr. Mackay found that cotton from India entered the European
' market only as supplementary to the American supply; for that,
' taking price and quality into consideration, it could not be imported
' so cheaply; and was received in any considerable quantity, only
' (1) when the American supply failed, or (2) when the demand for
' consumption increased, and, from one or both of these causes, the
' price rose materially above the average.''

From these statements it will appear that the welfare and prosperity of England as well as of the United States depend upon the
cultivation of cotton, and consequently upon slave labor. Millions
of men, women, and children, in Europe as well as in this country,
would be driven into a state of misery and pauperism, if our fertile
Southern fields should fail to produce the necessary raw material.
In short, the cultivation of cotton has become a necessity; mankind
cannot do without it. What would this country be without the two
hundred millions of dollars of cotton annually produced? Where
would be our greatness, our prosperity, as a commercial nation?
Let the people of the North answer these questions for themselves.*

---

* I annex here an article published in the London *Cotton Supply Reporter*, February 3, 1860:

"THE COTTON SUPPLY OF ENGLAND—ITS IMPORTANCE TO SOCIETY
AT LARGE.

"Upwards of 500,000 workers are now employed in our cotton factories, and it
' has been estimated that at least 4,000,000 persons in this country are dependent
' upon the cotton trade for subsistence. A century ago, Lancashire contained a
' population of only 300,000 persons; it now numbers 2,300,000 In the same
' period of time, this enormous increase exceeds that on any other equal surface
' of the globe, and is entirely owing to the development of the cotton trade. In
' 1856, there were, in the United Kingdom, 2,210 factories, running 28,000,000
' spindles and 299,000 looms, by 97,000 horse power. Since that period, a consid-

THE UNION CANNOT BE DISSOLVED.

There exists in Europe a confidence, among politicians of every shade and class, that the days of the American Union are numbered. The mistaken agitation of the subject of slavery in the Northern States, the dissemination of incendiary documents, the treasonable and blood-shedding foray of John Brown, and the assertions of William H. Seward that the conflict between slavery and freedom is "irrepressible," have indeed brought the Union to the verge of dissolution, and are likely to destroy the grandest confederation that ever yet existed. The happiness of at least twenty millions of white people is about to be exchanged for anarchy and confusion, our strength to become weakness, our commerce to fall into decay, and the rule of contending and ambitious States, like those of ancient Greece, temporary, unstable, and bloody, to usurp the benignant sway of peaceful and liberal institutions. In fact, it

' erable number of new mills have been erected, and extensive additions have been
' made to the spinning and weaving machinery of those previously in existence.
  " *The amount of actual capital invested in the cotton trade of this kingdom is estimated*
' *to be between £60,000,000 and £70,000,000 sterling.*
  "The quantity of cotton imported into this country in 1859 was 1,181¾ million
' pounds weight, the value of which, at 6d. per lb., is equal to £30,000,000 sterling
' Out of 2,829,110 bales of cotton imported into Great Britain, America has supplied
' us with 2,086,341—that is, five-sevenths of the whole. In other words, out of
' every 7 lbs. imported from all countries into Great Britain, America has supplied
' 5 lbs., India has sent us about 500,000 bales, Egypt, about 100,000, South America
' 124,000, and other countries between 8,000 and 9,000 bales. In 1859, the total
' value of the exports from Great Britain amounted to £130,513,185, of which
' £47,020,920 consisted of cotton goods and yarns. Thus, more than one-third, or
' £1 out of every £3 of our entire exports, consists of cotton. Add to this the
' proportion of cotton which forms part of £12,000,000 more exported in the shape
' of mixed woollens, haberdashery, millinery, silks, apparel, and slops. Great
' Britain alone consumes annually £24,000,000 worth of cotton goods. Two con-
' clusions, therefore, may safely be drawn from the facts and figures now cited—
' first, that the interests of every cotton-worker are bound up with a gigantic trade
' which keeps in motion an enormous mass of capital, and this capital, machinery,
' and labor, *depend for five-sevenths of its employment upon the slave States of America*
' *for prosperity and continuance; secondly, that if a war should at any time break out*
' *between England and America, a general insurrection take place among the slaves, dis-*
' *ease sweep off those slaves by death,* or the cotton crop fall short in quantity, whether
' from severe frosts, disease of the plant, or other possible causes, *our mills would be*
' *stopped for want of cotton, employers would be ruined, and famine would stalk abroad*
' *among the hundreds and thousands of work people* who are at present fortunately
' well employed.
  "Calculate the consequences for yourself. Imagine a dearth of cotton, and you
' may picture the horrors of such a calamity from the scenes you may possibly
' have witnessed when the mills have only run on ' short time.' Count up all the
' trades that are kept going out of the wages of the working classes, independent
' of builders, mechanics, engineers, colliers, &c employed by the mill owners.
  Railways would cease to pay, and our ships would lie rotting in their ports,
  should a scarcity of the raw material for manufacture overtake us."

seems to me as if we have reached a state of things, which calls
upon all who love the country and cherish the Union, and desire the
continuance of those blessings which we have till lately enjoyed
under the Constitution transmitted to us by the fathers of the Revolution, and which is the noblest work of political wisdom ever
achieved, to meet as one man, and take counsel for its preservation.
Talk of the dissolution of the Union! I ask dispassionately, what
has either section to gain by it? Will a bloody social war, the
necessary consequence of dissolution, remove slavery? Will the
cutting of throats and the ravishing of the wives and daughters
of our Southren brethren give any relief to our country, or silence
those political monomaniacs of the North? Will not every evil
which the North desires to remedy be confirmed and aggravated?
Will the South, on the other hand, gain any greater stability for
her social system?

Let us suppose the Union should be dissolved to-day. What
would be the consequences? Would the two sections continue to
live in peace, or would not, by inroads made by fanatical abolitionists into the Southern territory, for the purpose of inveigling the
slaves against their masters, very soon ensue a bloody war? Would
not the material welfare, the happiness, and peace, of both sections
be ruined forever? And in a case of war between them, would not
European influence soon be brought to bear against one or the
other? All know that this Union is the thorn in the eyes of the
despots of Europe, who fear that, sooner or later, our successful
example will be imitated by their own oppressed people, or that this
nation may become so powerful to drag them from their own shaking
thrones. And Great Britain, which spent seven hundred millions
of dollars to subjugate the American colonies, how would she rejoice,
if this glorious Confederation should go to decay! Some one may
ask, what has England to gain by a dissolution of the Union?
Everything. What seven hundred millions of dollars and large
armies and fleets could not do, will be accomplished by such an
event. She will once more come into possession of her best and
richest "colonies."

We are now her rival on the sea, and measure with her ton for
ton in the great race of steam and sail for the carrying trade of the
world. She knows that our shipping is owned almost exclusively
in the Northern coast States; she knows, too, that the best-paying
freight borne by those Northern vessels comes from the plantations
of the South—from the four million bales of cotton, from the sugar,
the tobacco, and other products of the slave States. She knows
well that the Union once dissolved, the most inveterate hostility
must ever after exist between the North and South. Being unable
to do without the cotton from the Southern States, she would assist
the South against the North with her navy; she would, with all
her power, prevent the North from abolitionizing the South, as such

an act would be equivalent to a cessation of the cultivation of cotton, without which her manufactories would go to ruin. France, which buys annually some twenty million dollars worth of cotton in this country, would rather, on that account, assist than prevent England from forming a protective alliance with the South. The terms of such an alliance would exclude Northern, and especially New England, vessels from the Southern trade, by the imposition of such onerous and discriminating taxes as would render competition with Great Britain impossible. England knows well that, in such a state of things, Northern manufactures would be excluded from the Southern market, through the agency of a high tariff, while British goods would be received free of duty. She knows too well, that, herself possessing these advantages, both Northern shipping and Northern manufactories must cease to exist. But what advantages would the South secure from such an alliance? The fleets of England would protect her on the sea, and the subsidies of England would support a Southern army, composed of Southern men, and commanded by Southern officers, to protect her from incursions from the North, or to pass the frontier with fire and sword, to seek vengeance for some unredressed wrong. England does a great deal more than this, for less advantages, in the East Indies. But mark! whilst the North would be materially and politically ruined, and entirely powerless,* the South would be nothing but a dependency

* New England, as the London *Morning Post* suggests, perhaps annexed to Canada! That my apprehensions are not so imaginary, will appear from the following article:

THE HOPES OF ENGLAND ON THE DISSOLUTION OF THE AMERICAN UNION.

[From the London Post, (Government organ,) January 3.]

" Within the last month, the Victoria Bridge, the greatest triumph of engineering ' science, has been opened, and the wealth of the Western States and of Canada ' will be carried along the Grand Trunk Railway to the Atlantic terminus at Port- ' land. Canada—thanks to British and provincial capital and enterprise—pos- ' sesses the longest separate line of railway in the world. It is, however, greatly ' to be regretted that this line was not continued exclusively through British terri- ' tory to Halifax; but this object we have a sanguine hope will be accomplished ' whenever that general confederation of the States of British North America comes ' to take place—a matter which has long engaged the attention of the people of Can- ' ada, and must at no distant day engage the attention of the British Parliament. ' If a war should unfortunately occur between England and the United States, the ' former would be excluded during one-half of the year from all direct access to ' Canada. *Again, if the Northern States should separate from the Southern on the* ' *question of slavery*—one which now so fiercely agitates the public mind in Amer- ' ica—that portion of the Grand Trunk Railway which traverses Maine might at ' any day be closed against England, unless, indeed, the people of that State, *with* ' *an eye to commercial profit, should offer to annex themselves to Canada.* On military ' as well as commercial grounds, it is obviously necessary that British North Amer- ' ica should possess on the Atlantic a port open at all times of the year—a port ' which, whilst the terminus of that railway communication which is destined to ' do so much for the development and consolidation of the wealth and prosperity ' of British North America, will make England equally in peace and war independ-

or colony of Great Britain! All the hopes and prospects which we now derive from the Union would be at once annihilated, all expectations of further greatness and power entirely crushed. The Goddess of Liberty would be compelled to leave the only country on the globe where she can show her face unveiled. The whole world would be shrouded in darkness, and despotism would reign supreme.

That is what the European Emperors, Kings, and Queens, are after. For achieving that end, they receive at their Courts the monomaniacs and treasonable political demagogues of this country, as "revolters from the camp of the enemy." They have no sympathies for the slaves of any country. They even are not in favor of emancipation, as they are too well aware of the failure of such a movement in the British colonies. Besides, they cannot do without the products of slave labor. Knowing that the political power of this country will be at an end as soon as the Union is dissolved, they secretly support any scheme which will tend to that result.

Let the people of the South remember that there are in the North two millions of Democratic voters, or nearly twice as many as in the South, who all love the Constitution and the Union. They are the great army that will meet, next fall, the British and American fanatics, who are now so anxiously striving to overturn this Government, and stop the source of all our happiness, prosperity, and greatness, the most precious inheritance we have received from our forefathers, the Constitution and the Union. Let all minor issues drop; place the Northern Democrats in a position where they are enabled to successfully combat the enemy. Let the Democracy, North and South, unite; for, united we *must* be, or we will be beaten. The Northern Democracy only can save the party from defeat. All the battles will be fought on Northern ground, for there is the enemy; you have no Republicans in the Southern States.

We have now only a population of about thirty million. But the child is already born that will see this country, if peace, happiness, and prosperity, should continue to bless it, number at least one hun-

---

' ent of the United States. We trust that the question of confederation will be ' speedily forced upon the attention of her Majesty's Ministers. The present time ' is most propitious for its discussion. Whilst the most distinguished men in the ' United States, such as the President and General Winfield Scott, view with natu-' ral *distrust and apprehension the agitation which is growing up in America in favor of a* ' *dissolution of the Union,* the people of Canada are quiet and contented under Brit-' ish rule, thinking more of economy and trade than of any constitutional changes ' which they know could not confer upon them a single iota of real liberty and ' happiness more than they now enjoy. But if slavery is to be the Nemesis of ' Republican America—if separation is to take place—the confederated States of ' British North America, then a strong and compact nation, would virtually hold ' the balance of power on the continent, *and lead to the restoration of that influence* ' *which more than eighty years ago England was supposed to have lost.* This object, ' with the uncertain future of Republican institutions in the United States before ' us, is a subject worthy of the early and earnest consideration of the Parliament ' and people of the mother country."

dred millions of inhabitants! No! this glorious Union shall not perish—this Republic, this free Government, cannot be a failure. Precious legacy of our fathers, it shall go down honored and cherished to our children. Generations unborn shall enjoy its privileges, as we have done. Posterity will class those who raised their hands against it, with the Arnolds of the Revolution. This Union and Constitution must and shall be preserved!

CONCLUSIONS.

1. The Republican party is using the very same arguments, and employing the very same means, by which, through the French and English philanthropical societies, the revolution in St. Domingo was originated.

2. Their efforts, if continued, must ultimately be crowned with the very same success, viz : bloodshed, murder, rapine, devastation, and misery.

3. Like in St. Domingo, it is not the slave population of this country which is anxious for rebellion. The negro slaves of St. Domingo were almost compelled to join the revolutionists at the first outbreak. Neither Ogé or John Brown, who both expected that the slaves would immediately flock to their standards, found their expectations realized.

4. The whites in France and England clamored for the abolition of slavery in St. Domingo, and not those of that Island itself. The whites of the Northern States, and not of the Southern States, in this country, do the same thing.

5. The philanthropists of the last century disclaimed any intention to interfere with slavery where it already existed.

6. Our Republican party does the same.

7. Although professing to leave slavery where it is, the British society for the abolition of the slave trade, which met at the Old Jewry in London, was, directly and indirectly, engaged to foment disorder and revolution amongst the slaves.

8. Our Republicans do the same.

9. History shows that the negro, as soon as he is left to himself, will, from an innate feeling of indolence and thoughtlessness, relapse into a state of African barbarism. Indigence, filth, and disease,

accompanied by a fearful mortality, are the principal and sole benefits he derives from emancipation.

10. That all southern countries where negro slavery has been abolished are, in every respect, utterly ruined.

11. That the negro race, not being able of taking care of itself, enjoys nowhere a greater amount of happiness and content than in the state of American slavery; provided that pauperism, sloth, indolence, disease, habits of savage life, idolatry, and lust, are not considered the chief attributes of happiness.

12. That four millions of negroes and eight millions of whites cannot live together in a state of equality; as it has been fully proved, not only on the American continent, but in the British colonies, that the enforced equality of European and African tends not to the elevation of the black, but the degradation of the white.

13. That a rebellion in the Southern States of the slaves against the whites would not only result in the entire devastation and ruin of the country and all its relations, but also end in the total destruction or expulsion of the negroes, after terrible scenes of bloodshed and rapine.

14. That the civilized world cannot do without the productions of slave labor. The destruction of the Southern cotton-fields would be a great calamity, not only to this country, but to Europe. Millions of white men, women, and children, would be placed in a state of utter helplessness.

15. That the apprentice and coolie system, a new form of the African slave trade, introduced by France and England, is ten thousand times worse than African slavery and African slave trade.

16. That the European Powers are not in favor of the emancipation of slavery in the Southern States, as they derive too many benefits therefrom; but would hail with pleasure a split between the North and South, as it would make both sections powerless, and remove the apprehension now entertained by them as to our future greatness and power.

17. That the relations, commercial, social, and political, between the South and North, are of such a character, that a dissolution of the Union must inevitably be followed by the direst calamities to both.

18. That only by a continuance of the Union, the political pre-

ponderance of the United States on this continent can be maintained.

19. That the advocates of the " Irrepressible Conflict," and of the "Impending Crisis," are the greatest enemies of the glory, prosperity, happiness, liberty, greatness, and future prospects, of this country; that their doctrines, carried out, must inevitably hasten the downfall of the Republic, and leave the people thereof at the mercy of the great European despotic Powers.

www.ingramcontent.com/pod-product-compliance
Lightning Source LLC
Chambersburg PA
CBHW020332090426
42735CB00009B/1513